IT Sustainability for Business Advantage

IT Sustainability for Business Advantage

Brian Moore

First published in 2013 by
Business Expert Press, LLC
222 East 46th Street, New York, NY 10017
www.businessexpertpress.com

ISBN-13: 978-1-60649-415-8 (paperback)
ISBN-13: 978-1-60649-416-5 (e-book)

Business Expert Press Environmental and Social Sustainability for Business Advantage collection

Collection ISSN: 2327-333x (print)
Collection ISSN: 2327-3348 (electronic)

Cover and interior design by Exeter Premedia Services Private Ltd., Chennai, India

First edition: 2013

10 9 8 7 6 5 4 3 2 1

Printed in the United States of America.

To my wonderful wife, Professor Marta Moore.
You sustain me.

Abstract

IT Sustainability for Business Advantage speaks to modern managers in all functions as well as to IT professionals. Implementing an effective IT sustainability strategy is essential for organizations pursuing sustainability as a means of business advantage and this book shows how to do it. The critical first step is getting clear about the ends of the IT sustainability program—the mission must be to further the company's sustainability objectives and strategic intents should include: (a) making IT operations as sustainable as possible; (b) partnering with other functions to leverage IT in making their business processes more sustainable and to grow the business; and (c) building a culture of sustainability within the IT organization.

The next step is to implement strategies to achieve these ends and the book explores the ways and means of doing this. These include industry best practices on how to apply the processes, techniques, and technologies related to Green IT and IT for sustainability (ITfS). They also include techniques for change management and building social capital, as listed below.

- Provides the basis for creating a compelling case for action in your company.
- Shows how various functions can and must participate in the IT strategy.
- Shows how and why IT can help formulate company-level sustainability strategy
- Provides a framework that can be customized for different sizes of companies including small–medium businesses, different industries, etc.
- Shows how to leverage lean, six sigma, and other similar programs in a company.
- Evaluates the potential value of a full spectrum of information technologies including cloud computing, carbon and water accounting, supply chain analytics, smart buildings, telepresence, and personal dashboards.
- Presents case studies from the author's own program and from other industry-leading programs.

Keywords

Green IT, sustainability, data centers, climate change, energy use, carbon, e-waste, small–medium businesses (SMB/SME), conflict minerals, life cycle accounting (LCA), change management, strategy, sustainability platform, environmental management system (EMS), intelligent buildings, IT for sustainability (ITfS), smart city, smart grid, smart building, green ICT, Green Grid, Green Datacenter, Lean IT, Carbon Disclosure Project (CDP), Global Reporting Initiative (GRI)

Contents

About the Author

Brian Moore is a sustainability strategist, enterprise architect, and lean six sigma expert at a Fortune 100 company where he leads an industry-recognized IT sustainability program. Since he co-created the program in 2008, it has generated more than $33 million in annual cost savings, reduced electrical power demand by over 3 megawatts, and addressed the full life cycle of IT equipment. With Brian's leadership, the program also built relationships between IT and other functions including supply chain, facilities, environmental health and safety, engineering, and communications; and leveraged the companies' lean six sigma, cloud computing, and social networking initiatives. Because of its significant results and comprehensive strategy, the program has been featured in a segment on CNBC and in articles in *CIO* and *Computerworld* magazines; had its strategy recognized as a best practice by Forrester and ICEX, and won five industry awards:

- 2011 *Computerworld* Top Green Organizations
- 2010 *InfoWorld* Green 15
- 2010 *Homeland Security Today* Green Information Technology Award
- 2009 Uptime Institute Green Enterprise IT Award
- 2009 *InfoWorld* Green 15

In addition to leading the program that won these awards, Brian has been an invited speaker at green IT conferences, has spoken at other IT industry events, and was a contributor to the book *Business Model Generation*.

His sustainability leadership also extends beyond IT. He helped form his company's cross-function sustainability strategy team, helped create its current governance model, and facilitated business segment teams that created segment-level sustainability strategies and business cases. He also works with non-profit organizations on visioning and sustainable business model innovation. He has a master's degree in interdisciplinary studies, and a bachelor's degree in chemical engineering. This breadth and depth of experience uniquely qualify Brian to write on IT sustainability as an enabler of business advantage. His online profile is available at www.linkedin.com/in/brianjaymoore/

Preface

Sustainability is not a problem to be solved, but a future to be created.

—Peter Senge

I'm up early, writing this in my home office before the beginning of my workday, while the rest of my family sleeps. As I write, the hard drive in my new Apple Mac mini hums quietly, but I am hardly aware of its sound or of the electricity it is using. My monitor is on and displaying this text, but were I not writing about it I wouldn't be giving a second thought to the power it is using as it does so. On a table behind the monitor I can see the laptop that I use for work and I note that a small blue light on it is pulsing to indicate that it is in sleep mode, and so drawing power though at a lower level than when up and running. Behind the laptop, I can see more lights twinkling on the wireless router that connects our various devices with the Internet. It has been running all night even as we slept and will run all day even as my family and I are at school or office.

In the next room, my wife's computer is most likely in sleep mode, but there is a chance it is running at full speed, because sometimes it does not power down properly. Next to it is our printer, drawing a small bit of power while in sleep mode with its wireless connection up and on the ready. Downstairs, in our family room, my son's laptop also has a pulsing blue light and so is using a bit of power. On the other side of the room, our computer-like digital video recorder (DVR) is drawing 35 watts—my son did a science project on "vampire power" and measured the energy used by devices around the house; we learned that the DVR uses the same amount of energy whether or not anybody is watching TV. Thinking about this reminds me of the various phones and e-book readers that are likely using a small of amount of electricity as they charge somewhere in the house. Not in the house any longer are the desktop computers that my son had before he got the laptop and that I had before I got my new Mac. A few weeks ago we took them to an electronics-recycling event provided by our city, so I trust that the lead, cadmium, and other heavy metals that were in it are not damaging the environment or making people sick as they break it down.

Even though my workday has not begun in the data centers of my employer, thousands (literally) of computers are running. The machines that provide the computing that I'll use during the day to send email, log my time, look at my paycheck on the intranet, or collaborate with colleagues in other cities are all on, as are those that schedule our shop floors, calculate our financials, and route our shipping. All of these computers and their associated storage and communication devices have been on all night, and are all being cooled by air conditioners to remove the considerable heat they generate as they run. In addition, because it is so important to the smooth operation of my company that the services provided by the computers are available when needed, a bank of batteries is constantly being charged so that, in the case of an outage, power can be instantly provided to keep the computers running until backup diesel generators can be started to provide a longer-lasting supply of backup power.

And, of course, at Google large banks of computers are running and being cooled out there somewhere and being cooled so that in the event I want to look something up I can do so instantly. Facebook and Twitter and Amazon all have computers running so that I will experience an instant response should I choose to interact with them. And at companies I can't even name computers are running to provide the Internet links that I will need when I hit enter and send my query to Google or connect via a virtual private network with my company's network.

How much energy use does this add up to? I'm not sure, but it's growing rapidly. According to a presentation by HP[1] on the need for energy efficiency in data centers, "today's cloud consumes the same amount of energy as the world's 5th largest country..." and "by 2016 large cloud/web services will require 8–10 million servers in data centers." A study that looks beyond just data centers by the Center for Energy-Efficient Telecommunications finds that wireless networking infrastructure worldwide accounts for 10 times more power consumption than data centers. According to the study, by 2015, wireless "cloud" infrastructure will consume as much as 43 terawatt-hours (TWh) of electricity worldwide while generating 30 megatons of carbon dioxide—the the equivalent of almost 5 million automobiles worth of carbon emissions, and this is a "460 percent increase from the power consumed by wireless infrastructure in 2012."[2] This is an astonishing growth rate. Five million cars worth of carbon emissions for global wireless use is perhaps something that we can accept, but if this volume of new carbon emissions continues to increase by 4 to 5 time every few years it will be the equivalent of 100 million cars within a decade.

At the macrolevel, then, IT uses a lot of energy and this use is growing rapidly, but the world is a big place and it is reasonable to ask how big of an issue this energy use really is. Five million is a lot of cars, but there are billions of people on the planet and it's sometimes difficult to judge one big number against another, so to gain a complementary perspective, we also need to look at it from the microlevel. I have not quantified the energy use required by my personal IT footprint as described earlier, but it is clear that the energy used by just the IT in my life is greater than the total energy use per person of the billions of people on the globe who live on less that $2 per day. As we look forward to a future in which all persons on earth have gotten to a decent standard of living and enjoy the benefits provided by having an IT footprint, and realize the population is on a steady path toward 9 billion by 2050, and remember that as much IT support as we have for our routines today it is likely that we will have much more by then, we can see that the global energy demand and resulting carbon footprint for IT could be quite large indeed. In addition to the energy use implied by this, as more of the global population begins to emulate the practice many of us have today of frequently updating our electronic devices to latest model, there will be quite a stream of e-waste generated.

Fortunately for the environment and for the billions of people who live within it, counter trends exist. Computers in the data centers at my company and those in Google's huge centers are more energy efficient and are being cooled more efficiently than was the case just a few years ago. At both companies, IT sustainability is a priority, and every day employees are taking actions that increase the energy efficiency of computing and manufacturers of the computers and networking gear are making dramatic improvements in the energy efficiency of their products. At home, thanks to better operating system software and to increased awareness on my part and that of my family, equipment is in sleep mode that would have been running at full power a few years ago. Also good news is that the stream of electronic waste associated with personal and corporate computing is being better managed. Individuals are becoming aware of the need to take advantage of services offered by their cities or companies in the area to keep their stuff out of landfills and companies are learning they must contract with certified processors to responsibly disposition their hardware so as to protect the environment and those who will be handling it.

The Other Side of the Coin

So this is a quick first person glimpse at the "footprint of computing," but there is another side of the coin we need to look at. At the same time that the environmental footprint associated with making, operating, and disposing of IT equipment is growing, the use of IT by individuals and by organizations to create sustainability is also growing rapidly. We can begin to see this by returning to the view from my desk as I sit and carry on like a typical knowledge worker. The wireless router behind me that I mentioned earlier, along with the Internet and the virtual private network and collaboration environment that my company provides will enable me to work from home today and be just effective as I would be if I were to make my 30-mile round-trip commute. This will save more than a gallon of gasoline, reduces the carbon put into the air, reduces wear on the car and tires, and frees up space on the roads, which are good things from the perspective of environmental sustainability. It also provides me an extra 90 minutes for productivity or for recreation and provides schedule flexibility that makes it easy for me to coordinate with my spouse on driving our son to school and picking him up afterward.

Similar benefits are accruing in a number of other households in my neighborhood for folks who work for various employers or who are self-employed, which I know from seeing them during the day when I take out the trash or step out to look at an approaching rainstorm. I also know from the occasional dog bark that I hear on conference calls that I'm on during the day that this is also happening across the world for many of the people who work for my employer or its partners, and by extension I can know that this is the situation for millions of employees of other firms across the globe.

In addition to reducing commuting, the ability to collaborate securely over the Internet will also enable many across the world to avoid business travel, saving their companies hundreds of pounds of carbon for each trip, and saving many hours for the employees. And, of course, similar capabilities are making possible an increasing number of forms of outsourcing across the globe. While there are clear downsides to both avoidance of business travel (fewer relationship-strengthening shared meals) and outsourcing (such as displaced workers and more challenging project coordination), the potential for helping people to flourish is immense.

Further glimpses of this other side of the IT sustainability coin can be gained on days when I do physically go into the office. If I ask for help from a friend in facilities, I can view the smart building systems that constantly monitor and tune the heating, cooling, lighting of our offices and thereby reduce our daily energy use significantly. I can also learn from facilities staff how they use IT-provided analytics to guide their energy efficiency investments so that they get the most energy savings possible with a limited budget across a large portfolio of facilities. Talking with folks in other functions would make other glimpses possible. For example, if I go down to the loading dock, I can talk with shipping managers about how they use IT to load and route trucks so as to minimize the amount of fuel used for each ton of cargo, while if I talk with an engineer, I can see the system they use to minimize the use of dangerous substances in their designs. As we shall see in the chapter focused on the topic, these are just a few of the great number of ways that IT can be used for making business processes more sustainable throughout an enterprise.

Returning now to my contemplation of my writing here in my home office, I reflect on just how much IT is helping me to create this book, which I hope will help managers to more effectively create sustainability in many companies across the globe. I'm typing on a computer and enjoying my large monitor, I interact with my publisher by sharing electronic files and email, and my research is so greatly enabled by the Internet and electronic sources that I can't imagine writing the book in a timely fashion without them. Moreover, I would not even have built the knowledge to contemplate writing the book were it not for my participation in the many flows of knowledge across the Internet in which I participate. Most readers of this book I suspect are also immersed in similar knowledge flows, even if they are not any more aware of them than a fish is of water. It's worth reflecting on how much slower our learning and creating would be without the cyberspace-based knowledge communities that we take for granted. The enablement of this "knowosphere," as Andrew Revkin of the *New York Times* has coined it, may be the most important means by which IT contributes to global sustainability.

Creating Business Advantage

This book is not just about sustainability, however. Its premise is that by actively addressing both sides of the IT sustainability coin, by minimizing the footprint of IT operations while also maximizing positive contributions, companies can create business advantage. (This also applies to nonprofit organizations, while they don't compete in the same way that businesses do, they can create the ability to better achieve their mission.) In the first chapters of the book, I'll systematically make the case for this and discuss how to do so in your particular organization, but here I want to provide a visceral sense for the opportunity by sharing my first person view of its size and scope. My hope is that readers will do a similar exercise for themselves and come to the conclusion that I have—that there is a big opportunity here.

When I ask myself for first-person evidence that sustainability can drive business advantage, the first thing that comes to mind is the concern that many people around me have about sustainability itself. I live in one of the redder districts within one of the redder states in the United States that produces lots of oil and gas and is no "ecotopia." Even here, however, the concern of ordinary people for sustainability is easy to observe and this struck me at a recent event. Our neighborhood has an annual Oktoberfest block party where we actually take time to sit and talk with each other rather than our normal practice of waving from our cars or from behind our mowers. It is always a good chance to get a read on what people are thinking about currents events, from national politics and the economy, to the local school system and neighborhood happenings, and when I attended this year's event a few weeks ago I was struck by how many of the conversations tied back to sustainability. In part, this may have been because I was thinking about this book and so was alert for the topic, but I didn't prompt for it and just noticed when it came up.

For example, I asked a middle-aged man who travels a lot if he was in sales. It turned out that he was co-owner and sales manager of a company that made new kinds of building materials that reduce the energy use for homes and commercial buildings and we chatted for a bit about the developments in that area and how his company was growing even in the midst of endless bad economic news. A similar "what do you do" query of the guy who lives across the alley from us resulted in the reflection that he had just left working for BP because it was so embarrassing to be part of the company that had caused so much harm along the Gulf. Another neighbor, a grandfather, talked about how happy he was with the solar energy system he had installed on his house earlier this year and how he enjoyed comparing notes on it with other enthusiasts in the area. Another grandfather, recently retired, told me how he really enjoyed having the time to be involved with a program that helped disadvantaged kids. New water conservation measures being enforced by the city was a frequent topic amongst the guys with respect to our lawn care, and, I could go on, but you get the idea.

Another source of first-person evidence is to notice my own reactions to what I encounter in a typical day. Yesterday, for example, I received an item that I'd ordered online and a label on the packaging materials described how they had been selected to be as minimal and as environmentally friendly as possible. I hadn't selected the product on that basis, but I found that learning about it increased my positive feeling for the company that I had purchased from. A less warm and fuzzy, but equally evidentiary example was the reaction I had to skimming this month's *National Geographic,* which also came yesterday. We subscribed thinking it would benefit our middle-school aged son, but I've since found that almost every month it has profoundly interesting articles related to sustainability and this issue's lead article focused on the plight of big cats such as lions and tigers. The pictures of the cats in the wild were pleasurable to browse, but the text was disconcerting—it pointed out that there are more tigers in zoos than there are in the wild and argued that the diminishing numbers in the wild are a barometer indicating diminishing ecosystems. Thinking back to previous issues, I recall being similarly disconcerted by discussions of the drought and water shortages in the western United States, by the impact of growing CO_2 levels on the acidity of the oceans and hence on the health of coral reefs and other sea life, and the by the news that the global population crossed the 7 billion mark as it glides toward 9 billion by 2050. Sometimes my reaction to articles like these is to discount them as hype from someone with an agenda, but more often it ranges from "that's a shame," to "that's a threat to my son's prospects for a good life."

I've begun to notice another aspect to many of these same articles, however, that invokes a different set of reactions from me. As I spent more time with the article about the cats, for example, I learned that there were people doing useful things about the situation. Not just concerned folks "raising awareness" and fund raising in hotel ballrooms, but special rangers that go out into the jungle habitats of the tigers and lions for weeks at a time to protect them from poachers. This aspect of sustainability stories leads to a reaction on my part of appreciation, and perhaps even awe and admirations, as in the case of the tiger-protecting rangers.

In some cases, however, learning about the positive steps that people are taking also leads to a sense of opportunity and even excitement. For example, when I read in Anthony Lovins' book, *Reinventing Fire*,[3] about how systems thinking and the application of existing or close-at-hand technologies has the potential to eliminate our need for fossil fuels by 2050, I'm struck by how things I know as an IT professional about technology, change management, and systems engineering can contribute to something big. I'm struck by the opportunity for my IT organization and my company to make significant contributions while also helping our company to flourish. And I'm struck by how it would be great at a personal level to be part of this.

But, what is the "this?" of which I want to be part? A phrase that I will use in this book, "creating sustainability," may be unfamiliar but I think it well describes the "this," the opportunity that sustainability presents for our companies and for ourselves. It is common to think of sustainability as the reducing of negatives, but the phrase "creating sustainability" reminds us that, as Peter Senge puts it, "Sustainability is not a problem to be solved, but a future to be created." It is like health—while it is good to avoid bad habits, to really be healthy we must create a healthy life style for ourselves and create strengths, and meals, and social interactions that contribute to our being healthy. If we focus only on avoiding or reducing bad things or solving the various problems that are a normal part of life, we somehow end up consumed by those bad things and problems. Reducing unsustainable or unhealthy effects is important and valuable, but not sufficient.

This book, then, is about the great opportunity that those of us who work in organizations, including companies, government agencies, city governments, and nonprofits, have to help them leverage IT to create business advantage by not only reducing unsustainability, but even more powerfully by creating sustainability. Business advantage follows from IT sustainability efforts because they address values that are of increasing importance to the many stakeholders of an organization including customers, employees, potential employees, regulators, shareholders, and neighbors. Helping organizations respond well to the concerns of their stakeholders helps improve their brand, reduce their risks, increase employee engagement, and offer products and services that are more in demand. In many cases, reducing unsustainability will also directly reduce costs and thus provide value to even those customers or shareholders not yet concerned about sustainability. This is an opportunity to engage in personally rewarding work while also helping your organization and making a difference for future generations. Let's get started.

CHAPTER 1

IT Sustainability Matters

This is the largest strategic opportunity companies will see for the next 50 years.

—Andy Ruben, VP of Sustainability, Walmart

The essence of environmental strategy is to make it an issue for your competitor—not for your own company—because you've already made sustainability an integral part of your business.

—Amory Lovins, Chairman, Rocky Mountain Institute

This chapter is intended to help you understand why IT sustainability matters to organizations and to their managers, and not just to IT managers, but also to those in other functional or general management roles. Before addressing IT specifically, therefore, we begin by recognizing that sustainability itself is important to leading companies and agencies because it is important to many of their stakeholders. An increasing number of individuals and institutions in society are making sustainability a priority and, whatever else they do, managers must ensure that their organization is responsive to the concerns of its customers, regulators, investors, employees, and communities.

So what is sustainability? There are many variations on how people who care about sustainability define it, but core to most definitions is the idea that we need to live today in a way that will not impinge on the ability of future generations to live well. Whether in the domain of the environment, the economy, culture, or society, sustainability means considering the needs of future generations when we make choices today. People across the world care about sustainability because they see how it connects with their values—with caring about their future, the future of their children, and the future of others in the world.

A common misimpression that many people have when they begin to consider the meaning of sustainability is that it is primarily a set of negatives—things that we should choose not to do or should stop doing. From "don't leave the lights on" to "don't dump trash into the river," "don't warm the planet," "don't acidify the ocean," "don't use up all the water in the aquifer," and so on, it is a list that just continues to grow as we think about the prospects of future generations or even of the future years of our own generation. Sustainability can be experienced as a long set of parental correctives expressed with finger waving and warnings about dire consequences. While, as we shall see, it is possible to hold a more positive view of sustainability, compliance with a growing list of social expectations and legal regulations is a significant concern for most companies and government agencies.

A related view, held by many, is that sustainability is about a big set of largely intractable problems. They observe, for example, that in spite of endless hours spent across the globe discussing the need to reduce carbon emissions, carbon emissions continue to rise—the United States, Europe, and Japan can't raise taxes on gasoline without hurting their economies, while China, India, and Brazil can't slow their building of coal-powered electrical plants without hindering the movement of millions of people to the middle class. Or they observe that the great aquifers in North America continue to be depleted even as awareness of their plight has grown—farmers need to water their crops and cities want to grow. Or they observe what is much in the news as I write this—the seeming inability of Europe or the United States to set budgets that will ease the tremendous debt burden that is being created for future generations.

Companies don't want to be seen as "part of the problem," and understand that they need to maintain their license to operate, so seeing sustainability as a growing set of problems is perhaps motivation enough for companies and their managers to have it on their radar screens. As a result, just about all companies are at least in the compliance phase of sustainability maturity, as described in the maturity model developed by Bob Willard.[1]

The real question becomes why some companies are motivated to move to the right on this model—why are some companies choosing to fully engage with sustainability with attention from senior management and perhaps even significant levels of investment? In many cases, the initial motivation comes as they discover that bottom-line benefits accrue from

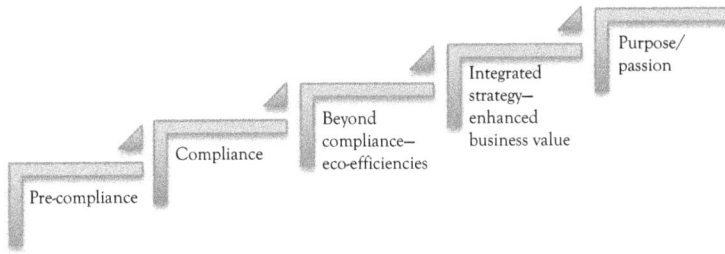

Figure 1.1. Bob Willard's sustainability maturity model.

developing eco-efficiencies—reducing energy use, for example, often leads directly to significant cost savings in addition to reducing the company's carbon footprint. Reducing solid waste, water usage, or toxic emissions can also result in bottom-line cost savings and as a company organizes itself to maximize its eco-efficiency savings it moves into the "beyond compliance" phase of Willard's maturity model.

Movement toward the next phase, "integrated strategy," typically occurs as companies realize that top-line benefits can be realized from sustainability efforts, in addition to the savings that come from efficiencies. Both consumer and industrial customers are increasingly likely to include "green" considerations in their buying decisions so that even if they don't pay a premium for sustainability when all things are equal, they choose the greener product or supplier. In addition, the markets for products or services in which sustainability features are essential parts of the value proposition are growing steadily and offer growth opportunities for those firms that can innovate to respond to them. Toyota's hybrid cars and Patagonia's shirts made from recycled materials are great examples of the reality of this dynamic.

So far we've been able to understand what motivates companies to move to the right on the sustainability maturity scale in terms of conventional thinking about maintaining the license to operate, and improving bottom lines by reducing expense and growing their top lines. To understand the motivation to move all the way to the right, to "purpose/passion," we must go a step further and look to the best thinking on sustainability that, in Peter Senge's words, views sustainability "not as a problem to be solved, but a future to be created."[2] In this view, which is shared by John Ehrenfeld, sustainability is not just about survival, but also about flourishing—"the possibility that human and other forms of life on earth will flourish forever." Sustainability can only emerge when "flourishing rather than unsustainability" shows up in our actions and that of our organizations. It is not just about protecting the future, but equally about growing today.[3]

A great example of this thinking and how it is driving creative corporate engagement with sustainability is the *Vision 2050*[4] report published by the World Business Council for Sustainable Development, a group of many leading companies from over 14 industries. This vision of "9 billion people living well, within the means of the planet" is concise but also compelling because it encapsulates the fundamental tension inherent in current trends and in our aspirations. Not only is population growth expected to add 2 billion to the total by 2050, many people are moving from profound poverty toward joining the middle class. It is obviously a great goal that by 2050 we should seek to have everyone living at a decent middle class standard with access to clean water, education, transportation, entertainment, medical care, and so on. The profound tension here, however, is that as people move toward the middle class, they tend to use more energy and other resources when, for example, they begin to own cars and air-condition their homes.

This vision sets up just the sort of challenge, "should you choose to accept it" as per *Mission Impossible*, that can pull your organization to new levels of performance and drive innovation across the board. New business models, technologies, processes, and cultures will all need to be invented and implemented in order to make possible a world in which many more people are living well while doing less damage to the environment than is the case today. Managers should care about sustainability because the challenges it presents will bring out the best in those organizations that accept them and send to oblivion those that don't. Leading indicators of this can already be seen as investors, potential employees, and customers are showing increasing preference for companies with strong reputations for sustainability and distaste for those with problematic reputations. It is clear, however, when we look forward to 2050, that today's indicators are only the just-visible portions of the large iceberg that is in front of us.

IT Matters to Sustainability

Having considered why sustainability matters to companies, we now turn to see why is it that IT matters to their sustainability efforts. Of course, in a mature sustainability program, all functions in the company must play a part, but what I want to establish here is that IT is of particular importance. Depending upon what business a company is in, other functions may also be of central importance, engineering in an engineering company to give an obvious example, but IT will be of special importance in just about all companies and agencies.

IT's Footprint

The first of several reasons for this, which we will look at, is that operating IT usually involves a significant environmental footprint and this footprint is likely to grow as more and more of companies' businesses are put online, automated, or informed by analytics resulting in more computing and online data storage happening behind the scenes. This behind-the-scenes computing happens in data centers—purpose-built rooms or even full buildings that are specifically designed to protect, power, and cool computers, data storage devices, and networking hardware. Data centers can best be understood as modern factories in which great quantities of electricity are brought in and converted into the compute cycles that are the basis of the company's business processes. Heat is generated when the electrical power is converted into compute cycles and so energy must also be used to remove this heat and cool the computers. The size of data centers vary greatly, but it is not untypical for their electricity usage to be equivalent to that of thousands or even tens of thousands of average U.S. homes.

In many cases, we can identify where a data center is located from outside the facility by the extra power lines coming in from the grid and perhaps even a dedicated substation existing just to effectively meet the power requirement of the data center. Also likely to be observable from the outside are massive diesel power generators that can kick in in the event of a power failure on the grid (or grids) and banks of air conditioning compressors or cooling towers that support the cooling systems in the data center that in turn keep the closely packed racks of computers cool.

In addition to this behind-the-scenes computing, an increasing variety of IT devices are being used by employees, each of which has an environmental impact. Desktop computers, monitors, printers, laptops, tablets, and smart phones all use energy—in many cases they use energy even when they are not being used, as for example when desktop computers are left on overnight and on weekends. These devices also generate waste streams of consumables such as paper, ink cartridges, and batteries, and at some point the devices themselves become part of the waste streams. Often referred to as "e-waste," discarded devices pose significant environmental challenges because of the chemicals and heavy metals used in their manufacture. They threaten not only the environment, but as famously documented in an expose on *60 Minutes* , they also threaten the people, typically in developing countries who must work to recycle them with inadequate protection from the hazardous dust and fumes that are released. These material can create places such as the one described by the *60 Minutes* narrator, "one of the most toxic places on Earth—a place that government officials and gangsters don't want you to see. It's a town in China where you can't breathe the air or drink the water, a town where the blood of the children is laced with lead."[5]

IT's Potential

The second reason that IT matters to the overall sustainability goals of the company or agency is that information technologies along with the skills of the IT organization can be key enablers for footprint reductions by other functions and by customers of the company. Whether through reducing the need for physical processes (such as replacing travel with video conferencing) or through using data and analytics to enabling processes to be more efficient (such as routing trucks on the most efficient routes), IT is often essential to improving the sustainability of business processes and operations. In addition, IT is essential for providing the visibility into the sustainability performance of the corporation that is timely, precise, and accurate enough for the leadership team to set and manage against specific goals and to confidently report on their progress to external stakeholders.

IT as Exemplar

A third reason that IT matters is that sustainability progress is a long-term journey that will require changes to the corporate culture, and IT organizations often have a unique potential to be a catalyst for such changes across the full company or agency. IT employees, by the nature of their profession, tend to be enthusiastic adopters of new approaches and so at an individual level the IT organization is a good place to introduce new norms. In addition, the IT organization is usually structured in a way that makes it possible to be an exemplar of new cultural norms. IT usually has contact with all of the other functions in the company while at the same time also being more centralized than most functions so that change can be relatively rapid within IT and so that this change can have a broad impact.

Summary

Key Trends

- **Challenges are growing.** Populations, CO_2 concentrations, ocean acidification levels, and average temperatures are going up.
- **Moore's Law is having an impact.** Networked sensors and computers are becoming ubiquitous as the cost of computing goes down.
- **Company valuations,** product selections, and employer choices are increasingly being influenced by sustainability performance.
- **Requirements for compliance are increasing.** Regulations affecting companies and mandates affecting agencies are increasing in scope and strength. In addition, unwritten social expectations that companies should go beyond compliance are increasing.

Principles

- **Sustainability matters to your stakeholders.** Make it an issue for your competitors.
- **IT matters to sustainability.** Leverage IT to improve the sustainability performance of your organization and its customers.

Additional Resources

- The *Vision 2050* report (http://www.wbcsd.org/vision2050.aspx) produced by the World Business Council for Sustainable Development lays out "a pathway to a world in which nine billion people can live well, and within the planet's resources, by mid-century." The report was compiled by leading global companies from 14 industries and aptly captures the challenges and opportunities for organizations related to sustainability.

CHAPTER 2

Think Strategically and Organize Effectively

Enabling IT to realize its potential for contributing to sustainability requires both strategic thinking and effective organizing. Strategic thinking is required to ensure that projects and investments are chosen so as to maximize returns and effective organizing is required to ensure that needed communications happen, that metrics are captured, and that ongoing planning occurs. Because strategy work in a large organization can easily become too abstract or too complex, this chapter presents a straightforward way to think about strategy that will ensure clarity. In addition, a strategic framework is introduced that will provide the structure for the rest of this book and that can also be easily adapted for use in your organization. To provide a basis for effective organizing, this chapter shows how to establish an IT Sustainability Program Office and suggests a sequence of start-up activities that will build initial momentum for the program. To ensure execution over the long term, another best practice for sustainability programs—the transparency, engagement, and network cycle—is introduced.

Thinking About Strategy: Ends, Ways, and Means

"Begin with the end in mind" is the first of Stephen Covey's seven habits and is also the first principle to thinking strategically. There are many misconceptions about what it means to think strategically and there are complex strategic frameworks in which this basic principle can be obscured, but here we will use the simple model taught to military officers[1] in which ends have pride of place. The short statement of this model is Strategy = Ends + Ways + Means. Or, to put it in a sentence, strategy is about finding ways to employ the available means to achieve chosen ends. An effective

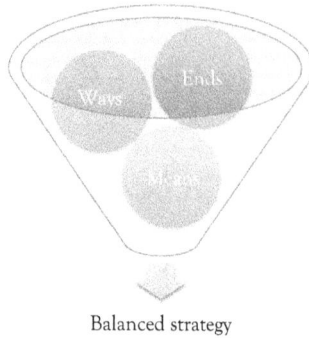

Balanced strategy

Figure 2.1. Developing a balanced strategy.

strategy results when ends, ways, and means are each addressed in a balanced fashion as illustrated in Figure 2.1.

Ends must be balanced with ways and means, which are also first amongst equals—strategic thinking must begin with consideration of what is to be accomplished by the strategy. Ends are objectives that if accomplished contribute to the end state desired by the organization for whom the strategy is to be executed. For example, the ends of a country's military strategy, if well chosen, will contribute to the peace and prosperity desired by the country's people. The ends of an IT sustainability strategy, therefore, should be chosen so as to contribute to achieving the sustainability vision of the company or agency of which the IT organization is a part.

Ends are best expressed with verbs—in the case of a military strategy this might be a statement such as "deter war" or "promote regional stability." Once established, they provide the basis for creating a strategy and mobilizing the organization, and hundreds of subsequent decisions can then be made on the basis of which answer best contributes to achieving the stated ends. Following this model, the strategic framework for IT sustainability presented in this book is based on pursuing three ends:

- **Operate IT as sustainably as possible.** IT has a significant environmental footprint that should be minimized as much as possible while still accomplishing the mission of IT.
- **Partner for sustainability.** The largest part of the footprint for most companies or agencies lies beyond IT, but IT can contribute to reducing it.

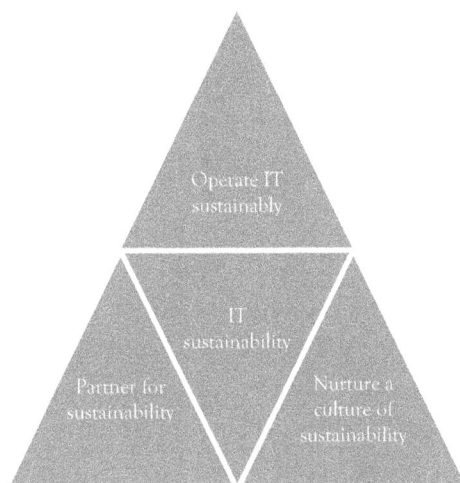

Figure 2.2. The ends of an IT sustainability strategy.

- **Nurture a culture of sustainability.** Sustainability cannot be achieved by a few silver bullets but rather is a long-term journey that will ultimately require engagement from everyone in the organization.

Once ends are decided, leaders can proceed to consider ways and means. These terms are used here to mean the same thing as they do in the title of the "Ways and Means Committees" in Congress. Ways refer to *how* something is to be done—they are concepts or courses of action by which the ends are to be achieved. In our military scenario mentioned earlier, for example, a possible way to deter war would be to maintain a forward presence of forces. Means refer to resources—with *what* should the ends be accomplished—and are described using nouns. To continue our example, ships or army bases are possible means of maintaining a forward presence of forces toward the end of deterring war. An IT sustainability example of this model is that a way of achieving the end of operating IT as sustainably as possible is to minimize the number of servers in data centers using the means of server virtualization technology.

Simply thinking through this model on a regular basis will go a long way toward ensuring that your organization has a vital strategy for IT sustainability, and in subsequent chapters in this book we will explore each of our three ends and their associated ways and means in depth. Prior to doing so, however, we will discuss how to organize your effort and introduce a process model to ensure ongoing effectiveness.

Establish an IT Sustainability Program Office

In order to fully develop an IT sustainability strategy, get buy-in for it across the enterprise, and then execute the strategy over a period of years while updating the strategy as needed along the way; it will be essential to establish an organizational structure to be the home base of this effort. A name for this structure that will work in many organizations[2] is the IT Sustainability Program Office: the term "program" conveys the fact that sustainability will not be accomplished by a single project, but rather by a series of projects over a period of time; the term "office" conveys the fact that while it provides coordination, much of the actual effort will be performed by other organizations. Note that though a "program office" may sound to some like it has a multiple-person staff, this does not need to be the case. Even in a large company, at least initially, the office may be staffed by a single person and perhaps use only a portion of that person's time.

The first order of business for the program office should be to publish an initial version of the IT sustainability strategy along with an initial set of actionable goals that can be accomplished in a year or less. In smaller organizations this may be just a matter of one or two persons "putting pen to paper," but in larger organizations, the first step toward publishing the strategy should be to organize a company-wide team tasked with developing the strategy. This larger team is needed because it will be important to have consensus across the various units of IT about the ends and at least the initial ways and means before moving forward. Without such a consensus, the effort to create sustainability is likely to collapse when the first difficulties are encountered.

In addition to helping to forge an initial consensus, there will be three other important benefits from organization of this company-wide team. First, it will provide a means to capture the current state of IT sustainability across the company, and it is likely that the team will surprise itself by how much good work is, collectively, already being done, which will provide a jump-start for the program. Urgent issues may also be uncovered, such as an area where e-waste is not being well managed or a data center that is over its redline for power or cooling. A second benefit will be that it will start the communications process—each team member should be tasked to communicate upward through his or her local hierarchy about the strategy work and to pull in information from those they work with to meet the information needs of the central team. As we will discuss further below, communicating is one of the key jobs of the program office and this initial burst of communication will be invaluable. The third benefit will be that the team pulled together to develop the strategy can be the basis of a standing team that will execute and maintain the strategy over the following months and years.

Responsibilities of the Office

The required activity level of the program office is likely to ebb and flow with the events of the year, driven by the rhythms of the company and by the initiatives spawned in pursuit of the strategic ends of the program. At the same time, however, there are several key responsibilities that will be constant:

- **Understand the business case.** The office should constantly be ready to present an up-to-date business case for sustainability in general, for IT sustainability, and for the particular projects and initiatives spawned by the program office. This means keeping abreast of the business and its market, of sustainability issues in society, as well internal sustainability issues, proposed projects, projects underway, and the results achieved previously. It also means being able to talk about the value of the program in the terms of the senior management team—financials, growth, risk, brand, market share, and so forth.

- **Communicate, communicate, communicate.** The office must maintain active lines of two-way communication with: members of the extended IT sustainability team, management teams, IT suppliers, internal customers of IT, other sustainability functions in the company or agency, and the larger IT employee population .

- **Capture and report metrics.** Showing the environmental and financial benefits that result from IT sustainability is an essential enabler of maintaining an effective business case for the program.

One of the real values of the program office is that by rolling up the benefits accomplished in local effort across the company, the collective benefit is material to senior management, and whenever possible financial metrics showing cost savings or cost avoidances should be highlighted. Metrics are also an important means of ensuring the projects are on track, identifying strengths or weaknesses across the organization, and identifying opportunities for future projects.

- **Update plans and goals.** Even while projects are underway and goals are being pursued, there is a constant need to "stay ahead of the curve" by developing and socializing plans for what's next. By the time a management team asks for next year's plan, or a project completes and team members want to continue to engage, it is likely to be too late to create new plans and get the necessary buy-in for them to be confidently offered.

Ensuring Execution—The TEN Cycle

Adam Werbach in his important book *Strategy for Sustainability*[3] provides a model for execution that is very relevant to achieving the ends of IT sustainability. He argues that a "positive-feedback loop of transparency, engagement, and networking," a "TEN cycle," is an effective counter to the "corporate killjoys to sustainability." The qualities of "transparency of information and communications," "engagement of managers and employees at all levels," and "a growing network of sustainability partners," he believes, work in a cycle to make for a sustainable organization. In subsequent chapters in this book, when we consider the ways of achieving each of the three ends of our strategy we'll identify relevant examples of these qualities.

Summary of Points

Key Trend

- **IT Sustainability Program Offices** or similar dedicated functions are being established at leading companies and agencies to ensure that IT is fully leveraged for the sustainability performance of the larger organization.

Principles

- **Begin with the end in mind,** but also systematically consider the ways and means of achieving the end.
- **Know the business case.** Always be ready to communicate the value of what has been achieved and of what is being proposed.
- **Operate IT as sustainably as possible.** IT has a significant environmental footprint and seeking to help other organizations without addressing your own will not be effective.
- **Partner for sustainability.** The largest part of the footprint for most companies or agencies lies beyond IT, but IT can contribute to reducing it.
- **Nurture a culture of sustainability.** Sustainability cannot be achieved by a few silver bullets, but rather is a long-term journey that will ultimately require engagement from everyone in the organization.

Additional Resources

- **Intel** was one of the first organizations to establish a program office for IT sustainability and a useful case study on it has been published. See http://www.edwardcurry.org/publications/ MISQE_SustainableIT_Intel_2012.pdf. There are also a number of useful references on the Intel.com website.
- **Sustain UCSD** is the sustainability program office at the University of California San Diego campus. While not focused just on IT, it's a good example of the role a program office can play in furthering sustainability in a large organization. See http://sustainability.ucsd. edu/involve/spo.html

CHAPTER 3

Operate IT Sustainably

Introduction

Operating IT sustainably should be the first order of business for a new IT sustainability program. IT operations often represent a significant portion of a company's environmental footprint. There are many opportunities to reduce IT's portion, and many of these opportunities will also result in significant cost savings. Moreover, the credibility that IT gains by addressing its own footprint will enable it to partner with other functions on reducing theirs.

Sometimes referred to as Green IT, this part of the strategy addresses the three primary environmental costs of operating IT:

- CO_2 emissions associated with energy use
- Environmentally harmful materials in IT gear including heavy metals, rare earths, conflict minerals, and plastics
- Consumables such as paper, toner, and batteries

In addition to minimizing the footprint of IT operations and laying the groundwork to work with other functions on reducing their footprints, in some markets progress toward operating IT more sustainably can be a means of top-line growth for your company. Solid progress in reducing energy use or recognition for responsibly managing your e-waste stream may provide reputational benefits that influence the purchase decisions of industrial customers or consumers of IT-related products or services. If there is a fit with your company's business model, it may also be possible to leverage the expertise that you develop in addressing your own footprint by offering consulting services that help other organizations to address theirs.

Start with Energy

Of the three areas of concern, IT energy use is where most organizations start, and for good reason. Saving energy saves money, mitigates the financial risk of future energy price hikes, and reduces the CO_2 emissions that result from generating the electricity used by the organization. The percentage of a company's energy usage that comes from IT operations varies widely based on the company's industry and its business model, but it is likely to be at least 20% and can be as much as 70% at a very IT intensive company such as an online brokerage. At the other end of the scale, in a company that uses a great deal of energy for manufacturing or transportation the percentage of energy used in IT may be as low as 3%–5%, though the amount of electricity used by IT may still be large in absolute terms. The trend, of course, across this entire spectrum is toward more use of IT, as services become a larger part of company portfolios and as all aspects of product life cycles are increasingly instrumented, analyzed, and automated.

In many companies, however, the actual amount of energy used by IT is simply not known, because it is not metered or accounted for as a separate expense. The energy used by desktop or laptop computers is seen as simply part of the energy used by the office space facilities, and even the intensive energy use within data centers may be simply rolled into the energy budget of the larger facility or site at which they are located. And as these data centers are often intentionally located where they will not be noticed, as part of their physical security, they are often not noticed by most managers in the company, and so their ongoing $7 \times 24 \times 365$ power is not on the radar screen. Even the CIO may not be mindful of the energy being used for computing because he or she is not seeing the bills. The same is true for water usage that may be occurring to provide cooling for data centers.

In contrast to energy costs, the capital costs of the servers in the data centers and of personal computers are likely to be on the radar screen of the CFO, the CIO, and other managers in the company. The IT budget is typically a large part of a company's budget and within that the capital costs for hardware are a large part. An easy way to get a quick estimate of the financial cost of energy used by the data center servers is to use the rule of thumb that energy costs over 3 years will approximate the lease or cost of capital for purchase of a server over that time. This will rapidly establish at least a rough sense of the size of the addressable opportunity from a financial perspective. The energy use of personal computers is less per computer, but in a company with many employees, the costs can add up quickly. One way to get a quick estimate of the financial opportunity here is to get the power rating of a commonly used personal computer, and then do the math to see how much it costs to run it for a year based on an average electricity cost for the company (e.g., 10 cents/kilowatt-hour) and then multiply that by the number of personal computers in the company (which may also need to be estimated).

Understand the Ends

Before launching the program, it's helpful to be clear about the target. There are three primary aspects to the end of operating IT sustainably:

- **Reduce the impact on the climate of operating IT.** In many companies and most governmental organizations, the largest contributor to green house gas emissions is electrical energy use and operating IT is often a significant portion of this energy use.
- **Protect the environment and human health from the impacts of IT hardware and consumables.** Because heavy metals and other hazardous substances are contained in IT hardware, it must be managed at the end of its life to prevent harming humans who work with it, and it should not be allowed to contaminate water sources or be dumped in landfills. The consumables associated with IT, such as toner cartridges, paper, and batteries, must also be recycled to the maximum extent possible and otherwise be handled responsibly.
- **Reduce the expense of operating IT.** Reducing the energy used by IT will result in significant cost savings that go directly to the bottom line. In addition, some of the steps taken to reduce e-waste will also result in savings.

Know the Challenges

It's also helpful to be ready for the typical challenges to operating IT sustainably, which include:

- **IT doesn't see the power bill.** In many organizations, the cost of paying for the electricity needed to run IT hardware does not affect IT budgets or the performance evaluation criteria for IT managers. Even though the cost to the company of the electricity used by

computer servers is likely to be as great or greater than the lease or
capital cost over their lifetime, this cost is likely to be out of sight
and out of mind for managers who have plenty of other things to
worry about that affect their performance ratings.

- **IT can't fully achieve these ends by itself.** A large portion of
potential reductions to IT power use can't be accomplished by the
IT organization alone. Whether in the data center or on the desktop,
IT may have to forge new working relationships with facilities,
supply chain, and perhaps human resources. And to address e-waste,
they will also have to engage with the environment health and safety
organization.

- **IT assets and operations are distributed widely.** If all of IT's assets
were in a single central data center, then it would be relatively easy to
ascertain the current state, set goals for the future, and then create
and manage action plans. For most large organizations, however, the
reality is that the assets are distributed across the country or even the
globe and are operated by a variety of organizations that may have
little contact with each other. As a result, simply ascertaining the
current state for energy use or e-waste management may be a
significant challenge and developing improvement plans will require
significant team building.

Transparency, Engagement, and Networking

As we discussed in Chapter 2, creating a positive cycle of transparency,
engagement, and networking, a so-called "TEN cycle,"[1] is a key enabler
of achieving the ends of sustainability. The ways that the cycle applies to
the end of operating IT sustainably include:

Transparency

- **Make data center energy costs visible.** It is often the case that data
centers are located within larger multipurpose facilities and that
IT pays for the space but does not see the cost of their energy use or
see the benefits that accrue from reducing energy use. When these
costs are made visible to data center managers and perhaps the
energy cost even becomes part of their budget, it is likely that

energy-reducing activities will quickly get a higher level of priority. Accomplishing this may involve working with facilities to install sub-meters; but this is likely to pay off quickly in energy savings.

- **Make sustainability characteristics visible** to those choosing hardware for themselves or their department. Many people will select hardware that uses less power or that is more recyclable if the information to enable this is available when they select equipment.

Engagement

- **Engage all employees.** Company employees make many decisions each day that affect how much energy their computers use, how much paper they use to print, and how their devices are dispositioned at end-of-life. Working with other functions such as communications or facilities to engage these employees in reducing their personal IT-related footprint can pay big financial and environmental dividends.
- **Especially engage IT employees** because they have an inordinate impact on IT operations, both with respect to the systems that they manage and with respect to them being role models for others in the company. IT employee engagement is addressed in a later chapter on creating a culture of sustainability within IT.

Network

- **Leverage your IT suppliers.** Many IT suppliers have leading company-wide sustainability programs and are often happy to share information on "how they do it" with their customers. It may be possible, for example, to meet with leaders of their internal sustainability programs or with their chief sustainability officer and, leading IT suppliers are primary sources of new developments that can reduce the footprint of IT operations. Great benefit can be gained by making sure they are aware of what problems you are trying to solve and by encouraging them to bring their innovations to you early.
- **Leverage facilities suppliers.** Also important from a networking perspective are the facilities-related suppliers including firms that

manufacture cooling or electrical equipment for data centers, design and engineering firms, and electrical or cooling contractors. The best of these firms are aware of best practices and are constantly innovating to improve upon them. They can suggest retrofits to your existing facilities and ensure that new facilities are built using the best possible options.

- **Engage with membership organizations.** There are a number of organizations that develop and share information related to IT energy saving. They provide good references and best practice materials for free online and have membership programs that provide more extensive information and other benefits for members. More information on some of the most prominent of these organizations is provided at the end of this chapter.

Organize and Align

Two critical success factors for operating IT sustainably are to organize horizontally across the various business divisions and subfunctions within the IT organization, and to align the effort vertically with IT and company leadership. Horizontal organization is needed to ensure that all the resources of IT are brought to bear on the challenge, to avoid redundant or conflicting efforts, so that good practices that emerge in one area are shared as rapidly as possible. Vertical alignment is needed so that the contributions of the initiative to the larger ends of IT and the company or agency are maximized, and so that the initiative is seen as making important contributions to the ends that leadership care about. The importance of this last point cannot be emphasized strongly enough. Any leadership team is continually required to make hard decisions about allocating their limited attention, people resources, and budget and will only provide ongoing support to those initiatives that make a difference to goals that they care about.

Horizontal Organization

The principle way of organizing horizontally is to organize a standing team coordinated by the IT Sustainability Program Office with representatives from each of the major parts of IT across the company or agency. The program office is likely to have little capacity to implement anything itself and will need to accomplish its work via other functions within IT. Therefore, in addition to the normal requirement of staying aligned with IT leadership, the office must be organized so as to stay aligned across the various business units or regional subdivisions of the IT organization, with several functional groups within IT, and with key functions external to IT. Examples of IT and other organizations with which alignment is essential include:

- **Data center and network operations** represent a large portion of the opportunity to enhance the sustainability of IT operations, and close coordination with the organizations that manage these operations is essential to realize this opportunity.
- **End-user services**—close alignment with this organization is needed to ensure that IT solutions deployed in the workplace are selected and configured so as to optimize sustainability metrics.
- **IT supply chain**—the IT group responsible for the process of selecting IT suppliers and products—is an essential partner for ensuring that sustainability criteria are taken into account in purchase or lease decisions.
- **Facilities** involvement is essential to working data center-related power and cooling issues and can also be helpful for addressing workplace or end-user issues.
- **Environmental Health and Services (EHS)**—close coordination with EHS is likely to be essential to implementing effective e-waste measures, as they typically manage hazardous waste streams of all sorts and may even have the lead role for managing e-waste.

Vertical Alignment via Metrics and Reporting

A powerful way to develop early momentum for a newly formed sustainability program, and to ensure its alignment with management, is to identify and begin to report a few metrics that will show progress and potential. The impact of reporting metrics can be very rapid because it's likely that there are activities already underway across the company that are reducing IT energy use, but the benefits of these efforts are not visible because the associated metrics are not being reported; there will be a sense of immediate uplift as the aggregate benefit of existing activities across the company becomes visible for the first time. Even in the case where no significant activity is underway, capturing metrics and reporting in place early will show this and thus help to validate value created by the program as benefits start to accrue. Deciding on and then collecting and reporting metrics are also good initial activities for getting the cross-company team to work together and will help them become aware of the impact of their combined efforts.

A key enabler of success is to identify the right set of initial metrics. There are a limitless number of data that can be reported but you want to find a small set that can:

- **Be easily captured.** Especially as the program is getting underway, there will be data that would be good to have but that are not readily accessible. For example, if metering is not in place, it will be difficult to report the total energy used by data centers or data center efficiency.

- **Be easily converted to business metrics** (e.g., money, cycle time). For example, electricity savings are often a good metric because they can be converted easily to cost savings by using an average cost per kilowatt-hour that applies across the company. It may be possible to use local energy prices rather than an average, but don't let the potential complexity of this derail the goal of getting reporting established early. Tons of carbon emissions saved can also be a business metric if the company is publicly reporting its emissions and has set reduction targets.

- **Reflect the activity taken by the program.** The scope of the program will grow over time and the scope of the metrics reporting can grow along with it. The initial metrics should show the progress made by the initial program activities.

The value of applying these criteria can be seen by looking at the case of a large multiunit company that had chosen saving energy in its data centers as the initial focus for its sustainability program. The "ideal" metrics in a theoretical sense would have been the total energy used by the centers and the power usage effectiveness (PUE)[2] of each center. However, while these metrics would have met the criteria of enabling the program to show that progress in reducing energy use could have been readily translated into cost savings, they failed to meet the first criteria of being easy to capture. The company did not have the data-center level metering in place required to capture total energy use or measure PUE, and installing the meters would have required significant investments by the facilities organizations. In addition, even if investing in them had been approved, they would not have been available for many months.

So, in place of the ideal metrics, the team identified two metrics that were relatively easy to capture and that would show financial benefits and illuminate action taken by the team. The first of these was a simple count of the number of servers that were eliminated each month by virtualization (an important technology that will be discussed later in this chapter). This count of servers was monetized by developing an estimated average cost savings per server that included the lease cost of the server as well as the annual data center hosting charge per server. In addition, an average value for power reduction created by turning off a server was set and thus the total power reduction achieved each month could be easily calculated. The resulting report soon showed millions of dollars in aggregate annual savings and thus gained credit for the program and helped focus efforts to do more, faster. Later, when the program had matured, their initial success provided a track record that enabled them to make the business case for investing in the metering needed to get more precise data.

Ways and Means

There are a myriad of means of improving the sustainability of IT operations and new approaches are continually being introduced. In order to organize our discussion and to provide a basis for organizing efforts in your organization, we'll look at four ways of focusing: on data centers, on IT in the workplace, on e-waste and the hardware life cycle, and on leveraging cloud computing. Each of these ways will provide a natural basis of organizing activities within your company and a lens for viewing the ever-increasing set of possibly valuable products and services on offer in this domain.

Focus on Data Centers

"Because that's where the money is," said a bank robber when asked why he robbed banks. Similarly, the answer to the question "why focus on data centers" is that for many companies and agencies that is where the energy use is. Today's data centers can be understood as factories that convert large amounts of electricity into the compute cycles that are the basis of an organization's business processes; for information intensive organizations such as banks or insurance companies, they can account for more than half of all the energy used by the company, and in just about all modern organizations, data center energy use represents a significant portion of total energy use. Focusing on data centers is thus an important way for an organization to reduce its costs while also reducing its carbon footprint.

Data centers not only use electricity to power the computers, storage, and network hardware that they contain, but also use it to drive air conditioners that cool the hardware and to continuously charge batteries or turn flywheels so that they can instantly provide power to keep IT services running in the event of a utility outage. Surprisingly, perhaps, it is commonly the case that the energy used by the support systems is as great or greater than that used by the core computing systems. A commonly used measure of this relationship is PUE, which is defined as the ratio of the total energy used by the data center to that used for computing itself. A PUE of 2.0 or greater means that the power used directly by computers is just one-half of the total data center power demand. While highly efficient data centers exist with PUEs approaching 1, most centers in industry and government have PUEs of 2 or more. For every watt used to run a server, therefore, it is likely that a watt or more is being used to keep it cool, bring power in at the right voltage, and ensure that power is always available. All told, the combined energy use of a medium-sized corporate data center often equates to that of thousands of typical households.

The good news from a sustainability perspective is that there are many well-established practices for improving the energy efficiency of data centers and many of them can be applied within existing centers at very little cost while providing rapid payback. Other practices are more expensive and may be tough to justify for an existing data center, but can be applied when new equipment is added during a normal refresh cycle, during a major refresh of a facility, or when a new facility is designed and built. Taken together, application of these practices can result in a center that is twice or more efficient than one where they have not been applied and millions of dollars of savings per year.

There are three main ways of reducing the financial and environmental costs of data centers: (a) reduce the energy used by IT equipment, (b) optimize data center facilities, and (c) choose "green" sources of power. Let's look further at each of these.

Reduce Energy Used by IT Equipment

When you tour a data center and see the massive facilities infrastructure required to cool and power the IT gear, it is tempting to think that the place to start in reducing energy in the data center is by doing something to make that infrastructure more efficient. It turns out, however, that while there is great value in addressing that challenge (as we will explore further in this chapter), the most profitable place to start is by reducing the power used directly by IT components. This is because of the Cascade Effect3 according to which reducing the power of a core IT component by 1 watt also reduces the power used by the supporting facilities by an additional 1–2 watts, depending on the PUE, so that the total power saved is as much as 3 watts.

Fortunately, there are several cost-effective ways to reduce the power needed by IT components and we'll now look at the most useful of these.

Consolidate.   The most direct way to reduce the energy use of IT gear is to reduce the number of computer servers running in the data center. This can often be accomplished by simply identifying servers that are running even though they are not still needed or being used by anyone and decommissioning them. While every server in a data center was originally commissioned for a good reason, it is not uncommon for servers to be using space, power, and cooling long after the initial rationale for their operation has disappeared. The application that they are running may have been supplanted by another application or simply fallen out of use, while the application development team may have moved onto new challenges and forgotten about the servers used for older applications. Finding these unused servers is not free; there are coordination expenses associated with involving all the parties needed to determine which are in fact unused and unneeded, but the return on investment can be very rapid. Turning off a typical server will save more than a kilowatt; when the Cascade Effect is taken into account, it can save a thousand dollars or more per year in electricity costs, and reduce carbon emissions by perhaps 10 tons per year, depending on how the electricity for the center is generated.[4] Further cost savings will be realized by reducing the occupancy, networking, and labor charges associated with running a server in a data center, and it may also be possible to eliminate lease costs or avoid a capital expenditure by using the server in place of buying a new one needed for another purpose. All told, eliminating a single server is likely to save $5,000 to $10,000 per year. If you multiply this by 20 or 200 servers, you start to be in the realm of real money.

Servers can also be consolidated by "virtualization," which is discussed in the following sections.

Increase utilization.   While most servers in a data center likely to be doing useful work can't be simply decommissioned, it is also likely that their average utilization is very low. Servers are typically sized to handle the peak load of their applications, but the actual load is well below peak most of the day and most days of the year. For example, an application that enables employees to log their labor hours is likely to be quite busy at the end of the workday but may be used very little during the day and perhaps not all during off hours. To take another HR-related example, the systems that support the performance review cycle are likely to be largely unused most months of the year. These examples illustrate opportunities because during all of these hours the servers supporting the app are being powered and cooled with little benefit to the company, and it is not uncommon for the average utilization of servers in a data center to be less than 10% and even as low as 5%. To put this in blunt financial terms, for every dollar used to power and cool a server, as much as 95 cents may be wasted. And the same level of waste applies to the money being used to lease or finance the server hardware, the capital equipment in the facility such as power distribution or cooling systems, and real estate leases. And of course 95% of the expensive labor being used to keep everything running may be being wasted as well. In addition to carefully sizing hardware initially, virtualization, orchestration, and utilization of the power saving modes on servers are means of increasing utilization, which are discussed next.

Virtualize.   A primary means of increasing utilization and enabling consolidation is virtualization—a technology that provides the "means to create a virtual version of a device or resource, such as a server, storage device, network or even an operating system where the framework divides the resource into one or more execution environments…. Devices, applications and human users are able to interact with the virtual resource as if it were a real single logical resource."[1] Virtualization can be applied to storage, servers, networks, operating systems, and applications to increase the utilization of the underlying physical resource and thus reduce energy use, the number of physical devices that have to be manufactured, and the potential for e-waste.

Because most applications in the data center are in fact being used, it is not possible to consolidate by simply turning them off and removing the servers they are hosted on. In many cases, however, it possible to eliminate the need for dedicated physical servers by replacing them with virtual servers. While a virtual server must itself ultimately be hosted on a physical server, virtualization software from companies such as VMware, Zen, and Microsoft allow one physical server to host multiple virtual servers that are from the perspective of the application indistinguishable from a dedicated physical server.

There are two big benefits of virtualization from a sustainability perspective. The first is a reduction in energy use—a physical server hosting five virtual servers has a higher utilization rate than would five physical servers because servers are sized to support peak loads but most of the time run at relatively low loads. In many data centers, the average server utilization is 10% or lower, meaning that 90% or more of the electricity being used to power and cool the servers is being wasted. When these servers are virtualized, their utilization peaks and valleys tend to average out. The physical server can provide the needed capacity for those that need them at the moment while the others use little computing resources, and while the average utilization of the physical server is perhaps now at 50%, meaning that the energy use for running the applications has been reduced by a factor of five—truly an amazing result with cost savings nearly as large as that accomplished by decommissioning an unused server. A second benefit from the use of virtualization occurs as it becomes standard practice for implementing new applications or for replacing servers when they must be refreshed. Reducing the number of servers that must be procured and then managed at end-of-life reduces the green house gas impact of manufacturing servers, reduces the e-waste burden on the environment, and saves capital and operating expenses. For technical reasons, there are some applications that can't be hosted in a virtual environment, but implementing policies and processes that ensure that the majority of applications are hosted virtually will produce substantial financial and environmental benefits.

Capturing and reporting these benefits will have the additional benefit of establishing the value of the IT sustainability program with IT and business leaders. In most environments, the total cost savings per server that is virtualized will be at least several thousand dollars per year when the cost savings such as leasing less hardware, using less space and energy in the data center, and requiring less labor to maintain are factored in. Developing a conservative cost savings multiplier to use in your environment and then reporting the cost savings achieved each quarter as you implement virtualization is likely to provide a powerful good news story for the IT sustainability program that will get the attention of even those executives who are not particularly interested in sustainability. For example, if your annual savings per virtualized server is $4000 and you virtualize 100 servers, you will be reporting annual savings of $4 million, which is a significant bottom-line saving even in very large organizations.

Virtualization may also make it possible to reduce the amount of hardware needed to achieve the needed redundancy and is an enabler of orchestration, which is discussed in the next section.

Orchestration.   Orchestration software "describes the automated arrangement, coordination, and management of complex computer systems, middleware, and services."[5] It enables energy reduction in the data center, allowing users of the data center to rapidly increase or decrease the amount of compute, storage, or networking resources being utilized for a particular application. When data center users can rapidly dial up the amount of resources for their application, they don't need to follow the usual practice of overprovisioning when they first stand up their service, and when they can easily dial down resource levels, they will be much more likely to do so after a peak usage period has passed. When this behavior is enabled for the many applications in large data centers, the result is likely to be a significant reduction in energy use due to the reduction in overprovisioning and higher utilization rates.

Enabling server power saving modes.   While the use of sleep states has been common for mobile devices and personal computers for some time, they have not been utilized in most data centers. In large part, this has been because data center administrators have traditionally been fearful of suspending or shutting down servers and thus putting at risk the ability to provide capacity when it is again needed. However, server hardware and software including operating systems, load balancers, and virtualization software have improved to the point where this option should be considered, at least for selected workloads. A server in a sleep state may use less than half as much power as an idling server and a recent study[6] found that total server power use in a data center could be reduced by 10%–100%. To help ensure that the use of power saving modes does not compromise the performance of the data center, companies such as Dhaani Systems are developing analytics-based approaches that model the usage patterns for the servers in the data center and then power them down and up again automatically so that they are fully up and running before periods of high demand begin.

Selecting components.   In addition to increasing utilization by the means discussed above, another great way to reduce the power used by IT hardware is to select components that use less power. One way to do this is to select less powerful components that still meet the requirements of their role. For example, IBM, HP, and Dell all offer servers that use lower power processor chips than are in their standard offerings. While the performance of these servers does not match that of their most powerful servers, they may be perfectly suitable for some of the jobs within a data center such as running the web server software that supports the interactions with end-users but that does not handle the application processing. Another way to select hardware, when less performance is not an option, is to seek systems that have been designed for energy efficiency and have features such as more efficient power supplies or energy management software and are likely to have EnergyStar™ rating. It is worth comparing energy use when picking IT suppliers and products, as the cost savings from doing so are likely to be larger than any cost differences in the products themselves. Another way of saving energy at product selection time is to select new IT equipment that can withstand extended ranges of inlet air temperatures.

This enables raising the set point on air conditioning and reducing cooling costs by as much as 3% per degree of temperature.

Optimize Data Center Facilities

While optimizing the IT hardware in a data center is the highest leverage means of reducing the energy used by data centers, there are also many well-proven ways of gaining energy savings from the data center facilities themselves. Some of these require only low-cost modifications that will have rapid returns on investment while others will require major capital outlays and will only make sense to implement when a new data center is being built or an older center is undergoing a major retrofit. We'll begin by looking at the lowest-cost approaches and then work our way up to the more complex and expensive approaches.

Raise the temperature.   One of the first things that should be considered for any data center is simply to turn up the thermostat and thereby reduce the power needed for cooling. Many centers are kept cooler than is required either by the computer hardware or for employee comfort; a good rule of thumb is that for every degree the temperature is raised, it will reduce the electricity used for cooling by 3%. This works just as it does in your home when you decide to reduce your air conditioning costs in the summer, but it is even more powerful in data centers because, typically while your home air conditioner may only run during the hot parts of summer days, a typical data center is cooled 7 × 24 × 365. A change of 2° would save $400,000 per year in a medium-sized room that uses 1 megawatt of power in a location where electricity costs 10 cents per kilowatt-hour. As the cost is near zero, the return on investment is nearly instantaneous, which is analogous to idea of simply removing servers that was discussed earlier.

This saving is available in many data centers because, for historical reasons, the temperature has been set much lower than is actually required. Earlier generations of IT hardware needed to be kept quite cool to prevent breakdown of their electronic components and so room temperatures were set at 72°F or below, even into the low 60s to accommodate this. Most modern server hardware, however, is designed to operate at temperatures in the 80s or above and so there may be much room for savings in a typical room.

Beginning in 2004, when they recommended an upper limit of 77°F, the leading industry group for heating and cooling professionals—the American Society of Heating, Refrigerating and Air-Conditioning Engineers (ASHRAE)—began to issue a series of standards that have steadily raised the standard upper limits of the temperature and humidity ranges for servers, with their latest publication[7] extending them still further. In addition to setting a recommended range, the latest standard also specifies "allowable" ranges in which servers can operate for periods of time without a serious degradation of reliability. This added flexibility enables some of the "economizer" forms of cooling, which are discussed in the following sections.

One needs to proceed cautiously, however, raising the set point only a degree at a time because there may be hotspots in a room that could go above spec (hotspots will be discussed later in this chapter) and non-IT hardware such as power distribution units or batteries that have lower temperature tolerances, and because comfort for the people who work in the data center needs to be maintained. In addition, as ASHRAE acknowledges, the optimum temperature set point is likely to be below the highest allowed point because as temperatures rise server fans operate faster and the chips become less efficient, resulting in offsetting energy losses.

Humidity set points should also be examined for opportunities for similar savings. Server specifications call for them to be operated within a certain humidity range to ensure that static electricity doesn't build up. However, if the range is set too tightly, the humidification systems will work more and use more energy than is actually required. Humidity is often added even to the air that is being cooled, whereas, in contrast, at home we may add humidity when heating in the winter, but in the summer we are usually glad to have as much taken out by the cooling system as possible.

Separate hot and cold air.   Air conditioned air is expensive and ideally it will flow directly to where it can be pulled through hot servers by their cooling fans. However, in many data centers this does not occur because before the cold air reaches its needed destination, it intermingles with hot air produced by other servers. This intermingling warms the cold air, reducing its cooling effectiveness and increasing the load on the air conditioners. When this is the case, a way of reducing data center cooling expenses that has a rapid payback is to optimize the airflow in the room so that cool air is delivered where it is most needed, at the air intake of servers, without first having been heated by the hot air that has been heated by the servers and blown out of the other side of the server box. In the worse-case scenario, no thought has been given to airflow and servers have been mounted in racks without any regard given to the direction of their airflow such that the hot air exhausted by one server blows directly into the path of the cool air being provided for the intake of an adjacent server. When no attempt has been made to separate hot air from cool air, the set point of the room must be kept much lower and the overall amount of cool air generated must be much greater than would otherwise be the case.

The most common way of properly managing airflow is to organize the racks of servers into an arrangement where the servers in the racks all direct their hot exhaust into common hot aisles and receive their intake air from common cool aisles. This "hot aisle/cool aisle" approach can be further optimized by taking steps to prevent as much hot–cool mixing as possible by means such as "blanking panels" that prevent air from going through spaces in a rack not used or filled by a server, by using plastic or metal sheets to prevent air from moving around the ends of aisles. These steps are very low cost and should be implemented wherever possible. In the case of existing data centers, however, migration to a pure hot-aisle/cold-aisle model may need to be accomplished gradually because servers running critical applications may need to be left running until a scheduled server refresh or other maintenance window occurs.

In addition to the low-cost means mentioned above, the value of separating hot air from cold air and otherwise optimizing airflow is so great that a number of other means have been developed. For example, wireless temperature and airflow monitors are available that can be deployed throughout a data center room and feed data to an application that provides color diagrams that enable operators to see hotspots or areas that are being overcooled. Sometimes this analysis can lead to low-cost adjustments in airflow (e.g., by changing the arrangement of the floor tiles from which the cold air flows into the room) that enable higher average temperature set points to be maintained or even avoid the purchase and operation of additional air conditioning assets. Another low-cost means of improving airflow in existing data centers is to ensure that the cabling under the raised floors or in other airflow paths is as neat as possible to reduce disruption. There are also a range of products available for more tightly managing the airflow within racks so that the cold air goes directly in and out of them rather than through the aisles. This approach is usually only cost-effective, however, for new data center constructions or at the time of major retrofits.

Leverage "free" cooling.   The next step beyond adjusting airflows within the data center toward reducing the energy needed to cool the data center is to increase the efficiency of the cooling air. One of the most dramatic and seemingly obvious ways of doing this is to simply bring in outside air. It is not uncommon to find air conditioning compressors running outside a building during a snowstorm because a data center in the building requires chilled air even on the coldest of days and no means exists to simply use the cold air from outside. "Air-side economizing" is the term used in the industry to refer to approaches of using outside air as a means of cooling. While it is usually cost prohibitive to retrofit an existing facility to enable this approach, it is often a very good investment for new centers to build in the ability to use external air during the parts of the year or even parts of the day when the external air provides sufficient cooling by itself or in combination with mechanically cooled air. In conjunction with the move to raise temperature set points, it is becoming increasingly possible to use external air even in hot climates during the evening hours and much of the day in more moderate or cold climates. The cost and energy savings from doing this are significant enough that companies such as Intel are actively studying the parameters for optimizing it and contractors are gaining proficiency in building the needed facilities. Water-side economizers are another means of cooling without using compressors. They make use of evaporative cooling or other low-cost means to cool the water that runs to the room air conditioners.

Utilize waste heat.   The air coming out of servers is heated to around 100°F–125°F (40°C–50°C) and it may be possible to increase the efficiency by putting this hot air to work. In some cases, it may be possible to use heat pumps to capture the heat for use in warming office space in the data center's building or campus. For larger data centers, it may even make sense to develop schemes for contributing to heating local homes. Other potential uses of the heat include heating greenhouses and swimming pools.

Power distribution.   Given the large amounts of power used in a data center, it is usually worthwhile to work with facilities engineering or external consultants to develop ways of reducing the inefficiencies associated with distributing that power. Opportunities include using more efficient power-related components such as UPSs or power distribution units, using higher voltages, using three-phase power, and locating as much of the power-related infrastructure outside of the room being cooled.

Data center infrastructure management.   Data center infrastructure management (DCIM) refers to a new but rapidly maturing set of tools that monitor and help manage utilization and energy use of both the IT equipment and the facility-related equipment such as air conditioners. According to the Gartner Group, these tools promise to "provide IT managers with energy and performance management capabilities never before seen. These tools will reduce operating costs, improve IT efficiency and enable sophisticated infrastructure analytics, extending the life of data centers by years."[8]

The reason for this great promise, as seen by Gartner and others, is twofold. First, they exemplify the approach of using IT to maximize the energy efficiency of operations that we will discuss further in Chapter 4. Combining sensors and other means of monitoring with databases and analytics provides a means to continuously tune the equipment to ensure the best possible operating results in terms of energy use. An example of the application of this provided by many DCIM systems is dynamic power optimization (DPO). DPO enables reductions of daily power use by servers (including the power used for cooling) of as much as 50%,[9] saving over $400,000 per year in a medium-sized corporate data center that uses

1 megawatt when at full power, assuming a price of 10 cents/kilowatt-hour. This is accomplished by enabling a migration away from the typical practice of having all servers always fully on to a practice of fully powering them only on demand. The DCIM system can coordinate with load-balancing or virtualization systems to power down servers into an off or sleep mode when not needed, continuously matching server capacity with demand. In addition to reducing energy use, these systems prolong the life of facilities equipment and thus save both capital and operating expenses by reducing weekly usage rates.

The second reason for the great potential of the DCIM tools, and what is new about them, is that they treat the large set of both IT and facilities equipment that make up a data center as a unified system. They capture and integrate data from all the various systems of the data center to provide a 360-degree view of the combined operation. Where previously servers were managed almost completely independently from the power distribution and the cooling required to run them, with DCIM the complete loop of power and cooling needed to operate a set of servers can be managed and optimized as a whole. A good example of the value of this IT–facilities spanning integration is the capability of many DCIM systems to capture and report standard integrated metrics such as PUE in real time. This metric is the de facto measure of data center efficiency, but is often not used because of the difficulty in capturing it accurately. Being able to easily and accurately capture this metric enables it to be used as a basis for continuously driving improvements. Some DCIM systems also have the ability to capture a powerful new metric: transactions per kilowatt-hour. This metric can be reported on a per-application basis, enabling IT to improve the overall efficiency in the data center during normal operation, and can be incorporated into server selection during the hardware refresh cycle.

Adopt best practices for data center facilities planning.   The European Union as part of its "Code of Conduct on Data Centers" has developed a set of best practices associated with the "utilization, management, and planning" of data centers. Practices here include:

- **Building the level of resilience in the data center only to the level actually justified** by business requirements. Often a data center contains an unnecessary level of redundancy, resulting in high levels of wasted energy to run duplicate systems as well as embedded carbon contained in the hardware. The amount of built-in redundancy can be reduced by providing multiple levels of resilience so that only those critical applications that need high level receive it.

- **Plan for modular or scalable expansion** in a data center so that provisioning and operation of excess power and cooling is minimized.
- **Design all areas of the data center to operate at variable loads.** This is in contrast to many of today's centers that operate at 100% in terms of power, lighting, and cooling regardless of how full the center is.

Choose Green Sources of Power

In addition to increasing the energy efficiency of a data center, the other way to reduce the environmental impact of powering it is to utilize greener sources of power. The most obvious means of doing this are onsite renewable sources such as solar photovoltaics and wind power generators. Depending on the location, this can be a viable approach to reducing or even eliminating the carbon associated with the company's or agencies' computing.

In most cases, however, it may be more financially efficient to procure green energy from a provider on the grid. If the data center is in the service area of a utility that provides green power options, then this can be contracted for directly, and when a new data center is to be constructed it may be possible to choose a geographic location that is advantageous in this regard. Renewable energy credits (RECs) are another means of offsetting the carbon impact of a data center. They enable the purchase of the environmental attributes of green energy that may be produced outside of the immediate service area of the data center and contribute to the overall reduction of carbon emissions by the larger grid.

Reputation enhancement is a possible benefit for your company that can accrue from your use of one or more sources of green power. For example, in the United States, the EPA's Green Power Partnership tracks organizations' use of green power and publicizes the top users in several industry segments. Some companies have also explicitly tied the marketing of their products to their use of wind or solar power. The cosmetics firm Aveda is a prominent example of this, advertising themselves as the "first beauty company manufacturing with 100% certified wind power" and featuring pictures of wind turbines in their print advertising along with models whose hair seem to be blown by the same natural wind.

Explore incentives.   In addition to cost savings from reduced energy use and reputational benefits such as those from green energy use, states, local governments, and utilities in the areas in which your organization operates may have programs that will help fund investments in IT energy efficiency. For example, the New York State Energy Research and Development Authority (NYSERDA) Industrial and Process Efficiency (IPE) program offers performance-based incentives to help data center owners and operators offset the cost of investments in energy efficiency and IT productivity projects in their data centers. Also in New York, data center customers in the Con Edison service territory can get help from the utility to reduce their energy usage, save on operating costs, and cut greenhouse gas emissions through more efficient use of electricity. Con Edison and NYSERDA work together to provide data centers with individualized and targeted technical assistance as well as up to $10 million in funding for energy efficiency initiatives that will generate as much as $8 million in annual energy savings.

Consider Cloud Computing

An alternative to making data centers more efficient using the means discussed earlier is to replace the use of data centers by "moving to the cloud." Cloud computing is one of the mega-trends of IT and for the modern world in general. In our personal lives, most of us probably use the cloud extensively even if we are not aware of it. Books are stored for us on Amazon, a seemingly bottomless supply of email capacity is provided by Google or Yahoo, which is always backed up, available just about anywhere in the world from any device and, for good measure, is free. Snapfish, iTunes, eHarmony, Dropbox, and so many more provide us services on demand with a high level of service reliability at low cost to us without our having any idea where the data or computing servers are actually located, how many there are, or how they are run.

From a sustainability perspective, there are many upsides to this ever-emerging cloud of services. It helps us to be more efficient in many of our day-to-day activities—online maps and traffic services help reduce the footprint of our travel, for example, and they allow us to be efficient in our computer use. The service provider has their computers on all the time and is managing capacity to be able to absorb our incremental load just when we need it and then return that capacity for others' use when we are finished, and, as a result, we don't need to have computers running all the time with low utilization in the off chance that we want to download some data to our phone or iPad. We also don't have to print as often or have hardware around to backup our data or have the capacity that would be required if we were running all these applications for ourselves. The significant downside of course is that the service providers do need to have big banks of computers running and they are building really big data centers as a result. Fortunately, the leading providers such as Google, Apple, Microsoft, and Amazon are working very hard to make their centers as efficient as possible and striving to locate them where they can access the cleanest possible energy sources and minimize the need for cooling.

For business IT, the challenges of adopting cloud computing tend to be much greater than in our personal affairs because of the higher complexity of functional requirements and the stricter and more challenging requirements related to information security and reliability. If we can't access our personal mail for an hour, that is an inconvenience, but if a factory is stopped or a company can't process orders from its website, the valuation of the company could be threatened. Nevertheless, there is a steady trend toward overcoming these challenges and adopting cloud computing by businesses because there is potential to improve business operations, as becoming more energy and resource efficient promises to reduce both costs and a company's environmental footprint.

Similar to what we saw when we looked at how cloud computing supports our personal computing needs, it has the potential to achieve high rates of utilization of computers by balancing the load across multiple companies, or in the case of a "private cloud" many parts of one large company, rapidly allocating or de-allocating capacity for each company, as it is needed, by applying virtualization and automation. The scale of the cloud service provider can also enable them to invest in making their data center facilities highly energy efficient and this is reflected by the fact that many of the world's most efficient centers belong to cloud service providers.

Though a detailed discussion of cloud computing is beyond the scope of this book, it is important here to understand the structure of the most commonly accepted cloud service model because it helps to understand the various ways in which cloud computing can be applied for business purposes. This so-called infrastructure, platform, software (IPS) model defines three categories of services that can be provided:

- **Infrastructure as a Service (IaaS)** provides the capability to the consumer (typically an organization) for provision processing, storage, networks, and other fundamental computing resources where the consumer is able to deploy their own software. IaaS can replace the need to have servers provisioned in a data run by the organization.
- **Platform as a Service (PaaS)** is similar to IaaS, but in this model the consumer can leverage programming languages, libraries, services, and other tools supported by the provider to develop or deploy their applications.
- **Software as a Service (SaaS)** enables the consumer (may be an individual or an organization) to use the provider's applications running on a cloud infrastructure. This is the form of cloud computing that maps most closely to the popular conception of the cloud and includes popular services such as Google Maps, iCloud, and Yahoo Mail. Organizations can also utilize services such as customer relationship management or invoice processing. Importantly, this is also becoming a popular means of delivering sustainability-related software services, as we shall see in the next chapter.

Focus on Workplace Computing

Though less concentrated than the energy use in data centers, the aggregate energy use from the many devices used in the workplace is also a significant part of the footprint of most organizations. From a technical perspective, reducing the energy used by IT in the workplace is a straightforward matter of selecting devices that are energy efficient, making use of the energy saving features on those devices, minimizing the number of devices where possible, and turning off devices or putting them in a low-power mode when they are not in use. The larger challenge for the IT sustainability program, however, is to find ways to work with other functions such as facilities, communications, and site management teams to ensure that these means of saving energy are in fact put to use and not disabled. The more that built-in, automated, or pre-configured features can be utilized, as opposed to leaving it up to busy employees to optimize energy settings, the more energy will be saved.

Personal Computers

The largest IT component of energy use in most workplaces is the fleet of desktop and laptop computers. Selecting models that have Energy Star or EPEAT (www.epeat.net) ratings will ensure that they are among the best available in terms of energy use, and so a key to success will be to work with the supply chain to ensure that when an end user or a department procures a computer, they are choosing from lists that have been preselected to have the desired ratings. Getting the value from these purchase decisions, however, depends on the next step. After the computer is purchased, operating system settings related to energy saving must be properly configured. Typically, IT can itself control these settings so that at least when the computer is initially delivered to the user, it is set to go into energy-saving (e.g. "sleep") modes when it is not being used. Depending upon the policies in place for modifying personal computer configurations, however, employees may be able to change these settings, in which case it will be necessary to work with other functions to finds way to engage employees in maintaining energy efficient settings.

In many companies, a walk-through the office area on a Saturday morning would find many monitors displaying their screen savers, many unused computers humming as their disk drives turn and their fans cool their CPUs, and building infrastructure working to cool the room in response to the heat being exhausted. When this is the case, turning computers completely off overnight and on weekends is an option for further reducing energy use that can be accomplished via employee engagement. There may be reasons in your workplace not to pursue this, for example, if IT administrators back up files or install patches and upgrades at night or on weekends, or unused computers may be used at night to support high performance computing needs, but if these concerns are not present, then just like with lights, using the on/off switch is a great contributor to energy savings. Those who may voice a concern that turning computers on and off will stress the computer and reduce its useful life should be reassured that this is not a problem for contemporary equipment.

A more automated way to reduce the energy use of personal computers is to leverage a power management product such as those sold by IBM, 1E, Dhaani Systems, and Verdiem, who claim that their products may be able to provide as much as an additional 40% or greater power savings.[10] Unlike built-in power saving features, they can address situations such as when a machine is idle yet unable to shut itself down or switch to a low-power mode. They can also be configured to automatically shut down machines during nonbusiness hours and automatically wake them up to perform maintenance, before shutting them down for the rest of the night. These tools also help to collect metrics on PC energy and can support environmental reporting. The downside of using these systems is that they add to the complexity of the environment and their relative value is diminishing over time as the out-of-the box capabilities of PCs continue to improve.

Another means of driving down desktop power use is to substitute "thin clients" for the desktop computers. These devices provide just the user interface for the user and rely on servers in the background to provide most of the computing, with the advantage that a typical thin client uses only 8–10 watts of power as opposed to the 60–100 watts of a typical desktop computer and monitor combination, and they can easily be configured to go into an even lower power sleep mode when not in use. In office environments with many workstations, this will have the additional benefit of significantly reducing the load on air conditioning. Additional power is of course used in the data center that is providing the compute cycles for the client, but computers running at very high utilization rates in an efficient data center are likely to use less energy than many PCs running at low utilization rates.

Other IT Equipment in the Workplace

Beyond the focus on computers, additional ways of reducing the power used by IT in the workplace include:

- **Deploying "smart" power strips** to reduce the power consumed by task lighting, computer accessories, fans, space heaters, and other miscellaneous plug loads in cubicles and offices. Many electronic products continue to draw power from the wall even when they are powered off. Since it's not always practical to unplug these items whenever you leave your desk, "smart" power strips can effectively do so for you based on either a timer or an occupancy sensor.

- **Consolidating printers** to save money by reducing the number of devices in an organization's printer fleet, and by ensuring that the remaining devices are more cost effective to own and operate. Strategies include the elimination of inkjet or other high-cost printers, the sharing of workgroup printers, and the use of multifunction devices instead of individual printers, copiers, fax machines, and scanners. Most organizations can achieve a ratio of one device (typically a networked multifunction device) per 10 or more users. Benefits include lower costs for hardware, consumables (paper, ink, and toner), electricity, and maintenance. If your organization still has non-networked printers in most offices or cubicles, or still makes wide use of stand-alone copiers, fax machines, and scanners, printer consolidation can save you a bundle. Representative savings run between 30% and 40% and can range as high as 60%.

- **Activating sleep settings on office machines.** Most printers, copiers, fax machines, scanners, and multifunction devices can automatically enter a low-powered sleep mode when inactive.

Focus on e-Waste

"Reduce, Reuse, Recycle" is a sustainability mantra taught in schools and it applies just as well to the life cycle of IT hardware in organizations as it does to the flow of materials through a household. At home, we can reduce our footprint by reducing the amount of stuff that we buy, using sustainability criteria as part of choosing what we do buy, finding ways to reuse items before discarding them, and recycling as much as possible rather than simply sending stuff to the landfill. Similarly, IT organizations can greatly benefit their companies and the environment by systematically looking at our choices across the full life cycle of electronic hardware, including servers, storage equipment, and networking gear in the data centers and personal computers, printers, tablets, and phones of the end users. From the perspective of IT, the life cycle of hardware begins with the selection of suppliers and individual devices, and ends with the disposition of devices at the end of their useful life in the organization. Each phase of the life cycle provides opportunities to create sustainability.

Supplier Selection and Development

One important way that a company can be a force for the creation of sustainability is by encouraging its IT suppliers to become more sustainable and the biggest lever for doing this is to include sustainability criteria as significant factors in the selection process. These criteria can address social and economic factors such as labor conditions in developing countries and the use of conflict minerals in addition to environmental factors. For existing suppliers, sustainability can be furthered through coaching in much the same way that companies have long coached suppliers on quality. It may be possible, for example, to work with a supplier to reduce the amount of packaging material or to provide take-back services to repurpose hardware at the end of its use in the company.

Supplier selection is also critical with respect to finding partners to disposition your gear when it is no longer of use to you. While an ideal e-waste program would eliminate e-waste entirely via application of the sustainability mantra of reduce, reuse, and recycle, realistically, it is not feasible to eliminate the need to dispose of electronic hardware, and so the goal must be to ensure that 100% of it is disposed of responsibly by certified vendors who are abreast of the scientific, social, and regulatory issues involved and who do what they claim to do.

Product Selection

The next part of the life cycle, which should be addressed when defining the end managing hardware effectively, is to select hardware that will itself have the least possible negative impact while still performing the needed functions. In the previous sections, we saw how much energy use and resulting carbon emissions are driven by hardware selection, but more than just operational energy use is at stake in purchasing decisions. Carbon emissions and water use associated with the manufacture of the device and its components, the consumption of rare earths and conflict minerals, the ease of recycling at end-of-life, and the eventual environmental impact of the heavy metals and other dangerous substances contained in the device are all factors that can be influenced by purchase decisions. These data may lead to picking one product over another and it can also help guide refresh rate decisions where the energy savings advantage of going to the newest model must be balanced with the energy saved by not consuming the energy embedded in a new device. Industry ratings such as Energy Star and EPEAT can provide a basis for product selection and goals can be set for the percentage of devices purchased that have the desired ratings. Where "bring your own device" (BYOD) approaches are used in the company, provide information to employees so that they can apply environmental criteria when they make their purchases.

The Use Phase

The waste stream can be minimized during the usage period by changing policies and practices as follows:

- **Increase the standard time for refreshing hardware.** Many companies have a policy of refreshing desktop and server hardware every 3 years. Changing this to 42 or 48 months will reduce a significant percentage of the volume, reducing not only waste but also purchase or lease expenses. However, this option does have some downsides that need to be weighed before changing policy. In addition to the obvious downside that it goes against the desire of end users to have the latest equipment (think of the lines to get the latest iPhone), there can also be a downside for IT if older hardware increases their costs for maintenance of the hardware and the software running on it. There are also two downsides from an environmental perspective. The first is that newer hardware tends to be more energy efficient and so slowing refresh cycles can slow energy-use reduction. The second potentially negative impact from an environmental perspective is that longer use of products may limit the options for reusing them (which are discussed in the next section).

- **Reducing the refresh of peripherals** is an option that avoids most of the downsides associated with slowing the refresh of the primary hardware. For example, most end users see little advantage to this year's keyboard, mouse, or power cord and they certainly don't use any less energy. Monitors used to improve regularly, but once the transition from CRT monitors is made, this is much less the case. And how many users actually do anything with the CD containing the user's manual? Developing policies and processes to stop the automatic refresh of peripherals at the time as the primary system is clearly a good way to save money and reduce the waste stream.

End-of-Life

The IT asset disposition (ITAD) processes should be designed to ensure that the environment is protected, maximum value is retained, and company information is protected. Options that should be part of the process include:

- **Redeploy high-end gear for less demanding applications** when it is replaced for performance reasons. For example, high-end workstations required by engineers or financial analysts may still be more than adequate for the needs of administrative staff when the engineers or analysts need to move to the latest high-end gear. Refurbishing and redeploying existing equipment reduces capital expense and IT administration, and supports corporate sustainability and financial management objectives.
- **Give or sell the hardware to someone who can use it.** In many cases, hardware that no longer meets the needs of the organization continues to function well and would benefit someone else. Options for doing this include working directly with a charitable organization, working with an e-waste recycler to have them donate where possible rather than recycle, and holding auctions for employees. In all cases, however, it is crucial to work closely with

information security specialists to ensure that hard disks and other memory devices are scrubbed appropriately.

- **For hardware that is truly at end-of-life** and must be recycled, the key is to select a recycling partner who will reliably meet the highest standards for protecting the environment and society while also protecting the information security of the company or agency. e-Stewards is an organization that certifies recyclers as meeting their "e-Stewards Standard for Responsible Recycling and Reuse of Electronic Waste" and recyclers so certified can be counted on to do a responsible job.

Consumables

Another aspect of the waste stream associated with operating IT that should be addressed is consumables—the materials used during the operation of the equipment such as paper and ink used in printing and the batteries used in personal devices. Though many aspects of the use of consumables will be outside the control of the IT department (e.g., end users ultimately decide how much to print and whether to recycle printouts), IT can still usefully set goals to reduce their consumption and enhance their disposition at end-of-life. IT can perhaps develop approaches to ensure that double-sided printing is the default mode and can work with facilities or other organizations to provide recycling of printer cartridges and make the proper disposal of batteries easy to accomplish.

Summary

Trends

- **The use of IT continues to accelerate.** Computing and network are playing larger and larger roles in both work life and personal life, meaning that behind the scenes more and computers are being powered, cooled, and disposed of.
- **IT is becoming more efficient.** The energy efficiency of computing is increasing exponentially. More efficient and reliable processors, virtualization, automation, denser storage, and so on are making it possible to do more computing with fewer resources.

- **Cloud computing is maturing.** As reliability and security improves, the cloud is becoming an acceptable option for a growing share of corporate computing.

Principles

- **Eliminate waste.** This lean manufacturing principle is profoundly applicable to IT operations. Once you begin to see waste such as cool air intermingling with hot air or servers running with low utilization, a constant stream of waste-reduction opportunities will present themselves.
- **Leverage the Cascade Effect.** Especially in data centers, reducing the number of servers in operation has a cascade effect on energy savings because, in addition to reducing the plug power of IT devices, energy needed for cooling, power distribution, and backup readiness are also reduced.
- **Reduce, reuse, recycle.** The maxim taught to school kids about the use of household products applies equally to IT products used in organizations.
- **Leverage virtualization.** Servers, storage, networking, and even desktop computers can be virtualized, thus enabling greatly increased utilization and reduced use energy and hardware.
- **Leverage information and automation.** Systems that capture information about data center facilities and about IT hardware operating in data centers or in the workplace should be leveraged to continuously optimize their utilization and, in many cases, this optimization can be automated.
- **Optimize utilization.** The closer to optimum levels that IT hardware can be operated, the less IT hardware and energy use will be required to support an operation. Leveraging virtualization, powering down unused devices, providing capacity on demand, and right sizing are key means of doing this.
- **Partner with facilities and EHS.** Data centers are IT–facilities systems and their operation can only be optimized by a close partnership. Facilities and IT must also work together to properly manage IT use in the workplace, while EHS is likely to be a necessary partner to properly manage e-waste.

Additional Resources

There are number of organizations that are doing great work in providing information to operating IT as sustainably as possible. Some of the most important include:

- **The Green Grid Association** is a nonprofit, open industry consortium of end users, policy makers, technology providers, facility architects, and utility companies that works to improve the resource efficiency of IT and data centers throughout the world. The Green Grid "seeks to unite global industry efforts, create a common set of metrics, and develop technical resources and educational tools to further its goals." In addition to publishing great materials, they provide a means for IT practitioners to share information with each other across company and industry boundaries. www.greengrid.org

- **United States EPA's Energy Star** programs include the Data Center Energy Efficiency Initiative that works with the IT industry to identify ways in which energy efficiency can be measured, documented, and implemented in data centers. The agency also provides information on how to reduce energy use through peripheral programs and by recycling electronics.

- **American Society of Heating, Refrigeration and Air Conditioning Engineers (ASHRAE)**—Its technical Committee 9.9 focuses on mission critical facilities, technology spaces, and electronic equipment. They are the leading organization in establishing and publishing standards for the temperature and humidity requirements for data centers and provide research-based best practices for energy-efficient cooling.

- **The Data Center Energy Efficiency Framework (DCEEF)** was created through an Innovation Grant from New York State and seeks to assist data center owners with a set of remediation plans based on end-user validated programs that reduce CAPEX and OPEX relative to power consumption. Each year they add data, solutions, and additional best practices. Over 80 individuals and 40 Fortune 500 firms participated in the creation of the DCEEF and the data come directly from the owner/operators community. This unique end-user driven experiment looks to create a "cookbook" of best practices that span any activity, procedure, technology, or policy that can assist in the reduction of energy use or carbon reduction.

- **The e-Stewards Initiative** (e-stewards.org) is a project of the Basel Action Network, which is a nonprofit that provides global leadership for addressing the human and environmental impacts of toxic materials. The e-Stewards certification program for electronics recyclers is "creating a network of responsible collection and processing entities, ensuring businesses and consumers alike that their old technology will not poison vulnerable populations, recycling workers or the global ecosystem." They also enable users of electronics to enroll as an "e-Stewards Enterprise" that is publicly committed to use e-Stewards Certified Recyclers for your electronic waste management when possible.

CHAPTER 4

Partner for Sustainability

In order for a company or agency to be a leader in sustainability, it is imperative that IT partner with other functions to create better sustainability performance within and across the various business processes of the enterprise. Within each function or cross-functional process, there are three dimensions along which IT can contribute to better sustainability performance:

- Support for decision making
- Support for social capital creation
- Support for replacing "atoms with bits"

Support for decision making is key because creating sustainability is largely a process of decision making. Whether at the scale of an individual making a decision about which car to buy or which container to recycle or at the level of an executive structuring a supply chain, the extent to which sustainability is created or destroyed is determined by a series of decisions. The initial decision to "be more sustainable" is just the beginning of the decision making that will proceed from then onward about the choices that present themselves on a daily basis. While some of these choices will be black and white—whether to dump used electronics in a field, for example—others will be less so. A company may have hundreds of ideas for sustainability-improving investments, but given a limited budget, which ones should it actually make in order to do the most good? A shipper knows that fuel use per ton-mile is reduced when its trucks are as fully loaded as possible, but how does it accomplish this while still getting shipments out on a timely basis? A building manager recognizes the need to remove the waste involved in heating and cooling a building, but how can this be accomplished without diminishing the comfort of the occupants?

Just about all of these "how to do it" questions are more likely to be well answered when informed by good information. In some cases, the needed information may be such that it can be obtained from a reference in a library—such as a *Consumer Reports* assessment of hybrid cars. But in many cases, information about the particular situation in which the decision maker must decide is required—such as the expected environmental and financial returns of the investment opportunities presented to the funding committee. Providing information to decision makers at all levels, whether it be reference material or real-time information is, of course, a large part of the reason IT exists. Effective IT solutions have long been recognized as essential to effective decision making in finance, HR, engineering, supply chain, and in the boardroom. And this is just as true for those employees working on the factory floor or facing the customer as it is for those in the executive suites. As sustainability becomes an objective for the organization, the need for IT support for sustainability across the enterprise becomes as much of an imperative as is IT support for finance making, quality, customer service, or engineering excellence.

Another key driver of sustainability performance is social capital—knowledge sharing, discussion, team and community building, and so on are essential to the journey of sustainability. The power of IT platforms to support these ends is evidenced regularly in news stories about various social, cultural, and political movements around the world that are being enabled by services such as Twitter and Facebook. Similar services can now be hosted for internal use by organizations.

Dematerializing processes, moving from "atoms to bits," is the third dimension along which IT can enable sustainability. For example, replacing air travel with teleconferencing for a business meeting has a big net greenhouse gas (GHG) reduction and using computer-aided engineering tools to create multiple models prior to building the first prototype of a car greatly reduces the amount of materials used. Other common examples include replacing paper billing with electronic means and providing maintenance manuals on a tablet or laptop.

A Note on the Use of Spreadsheets

Once it is accepted that information is needed to support decision making in an area of concern, the next question is usually whether the needed information can be provided without any dedicated systems, using only existing general purpose tools such as spreadsheets and email. Will the functions involved need to engage with the IT department to provide applications and databases? Or, will they be able to "roll their own" using their office applications?

While the answers to these questions will vary based on the size of the organization or the function within an larger organization, it is certainly the case that when organizations first start to address sustainability issues such as energy use, water, solid waste, and carbon emissions, they naturally begin by developing spreadsheets and sharing them via email. There is a good reason that spreadsheets and email were the original "killer apps" and their use will help organizations to make rapid initial progress in getting their arms around their sustainability data.

However, all but the simplest or smallest of organizations are likely to find that at some point their sustainability progress is hindered by the limitations of informal methods based on spreadsheets and that the expense of maintaining accurate information in them is larger than the expense of migrating to purpose-built systems. Just as the CFO does not want cash management to be subject to the delays and risk of error inherent in a spreadsheet-based approach, so too those in charge of managing the sustainability performance of the company are likely to find that the accuracy, precision, timeliness, and granularity of sustainability-related information needed across the organization to support effective decision making cannot be affordably achieved with only spreadsheets.

Of course, organizations have also learned, often at great expense, the counterlesson that a great "IT system in the sky" is not a guarantor of improved results and can even be a hindrance. Manufacturers have been hindered in adopting lean methods by their manufacturing resource planning systems, and hospitals have seen expensive electronic medical record systems obstruct patient care. What is needed to support sustainability goals, just as is the case with other organizational objectives, is an Occam's razor approach of keeping things as simple as possible, but not any simpler than is in fact needed. This is a nontrivial challenge, but the good news is that sustainability efforts have the advantage that they can learn from the trial and errors of previous waves of IT applications and from hard-won lessons learned.

Another element of good news is that as sustainability has grown more prominent as a concern of companies and agencies, the IT industry has identified this concern as a market opportunity. Established IT heavyweights such as Microsoft, SAP, CA, and IBM have multiple offerings that leverage technology they've developed for other purposes and that to various extents integrate with their other solutions. At the same time, companies focused specifically on software and services related to sustainability such as Hara, C3, and Enablon are developing integrated solutions that leverage their knowledge of sustainability issues. In addition, hundreds of companies are developing individual applications or devices that address a specific sustainability challenge. These range from low-cost apps for smartphones that help consumers to reduce their energy use at home to expensive, sophisticated systems that help utilities better manage the power grid or help airlines reduce the fuel used by planes as they approach the runway for landing.

Challenges

As with most endeavors to introduce new uses of IT in an organization, there are business and cultural challenges that must be addressed in addition to the technology issues. Typical challenges to establishing IT as a partner for sustainability within a company or agency include:

- **Making the business case** for new IT investments (and making the case for sustainability). In most areas, sustainability-related work is being accomplished today using a combination of spreadsheets, homegrown databases, specialized applications, and email. Making the case to invest in enterprise-class systems too will have to overcome the logical "it's not broken" line of thought not only by showing how doing so will improve the productivity using the current tools, but also by showing how new systems will make the company itself more efficient, profitable, and sustainable. The challenge of making the business case for sustainability-related systems is likely to overlap with the need to make the business case for sustainability itself. Systems can only be justified on the basis that they increase sustainability if the value of doing so has been established.

- **Organizations may be threatened by overtures from IT.** For example, energy engineers may perceive offers of help from IT as slights to their competence—"don't they know that we've been successfully reducing energy use for years?" This challenge can be addressed by patiently building trust by, for example, showing appreciation for accomplishments and talents of those doing the work of sustainability today.

- **The features of sustainability-related IT systems overlap.** The sustainability-related requirements of the organization are likely to be beyond the scope of any one system, but at the same time, many of the available systems are likely to have a range of functionality that overlaps with that of other needed systems. This is true for many applications of IT, but especially so for sustainability as it is a relatively new domain and the conventions and standardization typical of more mature areas such as manufacturing resource planning have not yet been developed.

- **Optimizing sustainability can introduce security threats.** Using external, cloud-based services to monitor and control heating and cooling systems, water use, or power distribution can be a great way to rapidly improve efficiencies while minimizing investment in conventional IT infrastructure. A concern that must be addressed when doing so, however, is that opening the control of mechanical elements to external sources introduces a security risk—nefarious forces may seek to hijack the control to hurt the company or agency. As opposed to "typical" computer hacking that only affects information systems, a hack of these systems could turn off power, disable a factory, or damage mechanical systems.

- **Getting the data.** In order for IT systems to provide reporting and analytical services related to energy or water use, they need to have access to the underlying data. In a large organization with facilities in many locations, this will mean pulling together information from numerous utilities that bill at different times and that are paid by different organizations using different systems. Another challenge is that many facilities lack "submetering"—that is, they have meters that show how much energy or water is used by the whole facility but don't have the ability to see how much is being used by segments within the facility such as manufacturing lines, data centers, or individual floors or modules.

Organize and Align

The IT Sustainability Program Office is likely to have little capacity to implement anything itself, but will accomplish its work via other functions within IT. Therefore, in addition to the normal requirement of staying aligned with IT leadership, the office must be organized so as to stay aligned with the functions within IT that establish and execute the detailed plans for the organization. Examples of IT organizations with which alignment is essential include:

- **Enterprise architecture.** It will be important to ensure that sustainability-related solutions are developed so as to make maximum use of the rest of the IT environment and not hinder the goals of the architects to continually simplify the environment or conflict with any architectural standards or principles.
- **IT security.** Close alignment and coordination with IT security is essential because some of the solutions emerging to support sustainability goals raise security concerns. For example, a cloud-based means of optimizing the energy use by company facilities may expose the company to attacks, which result in facilities' power being turned off or equipment being damaged.
- **Enterprise applications.** The applications team has existing relationships with the organizations now focusing on sustainability and probably also has existing roadmaps and plans for supporting them. New sustainability-related requirements need to become part of the discussions between the applications teams and their customers and sustainability-related systems implementations need to become integrated into the roadmaps.

Alignment must also be established beyond IT with the organizations that set the direction for sustainability in the company or agency. These may include:

- **The chief sustainability officer's (CSO's) office**, when an organization is fortunate to have one, will be a primary customer of IT services that help them to measure and track sustainability goals and performance. They will also be involved in conversations about how the company might want to change its business model to gain business advantage related to sustainability and thus can help IT to be at the table and contribute to those discussions.

- **Sustainability program offices in other functions**, when they exist, will be essential partners for understanding how IT can contribute to sustainability in their functions. Maintaining close relationships with other program offices is also a great way to participate in conversations that shape the sustainability strategy of the enterprise.
- **Sustainability offices within business units,** when they exist, can be an excellent means of ensuring that IT is supporting efforts to make business processes more sustainable. They are also likely to be a means of participating in discussions about new business models that further sustainability.

TEN Cycle

The cycle of transparency, engagement, and networking (TEN) we discussed with respect IT operations is also helpful for shaping our thinking about how to partner for sustainability. Guidance suggested by the goal of a positive TEN cycle includes:

Transparency

A key principle for designing IT systems to support sustainability is to ensure that they contribute to the transparency of the underlying data. Internally, this means ensuring that those who are making decisions that drive energy use can see the impacts of those decisions. Externally, this means supporting the sustainability reporting of the company and may also mean providing direct access to some data for public access.

Engagement

A key to success in deploying IT systems that support sustainability is to engage with the various stakeholders of the systems, especially those who will be using the information provided by the systems, but those who will be adding information to the system also need to be able to make the system work for them. If these stakeholders do not feel that it is their system, but just something from IT, or if they don't feel it enables them to make contributions to sustainability objectives, it is unlikely that the system will be a success. Another aspect of engagement is that, as we will see, IT systems can contribute to efforts to promote employee engagement with sustainability.

Networking

Sustainability software suppliers provide an opportunity for building a valuable network. They not only have information about their current and planned software offerings, but also have great information about what their other customers are doing. They may even have a users group or other forums in which to interact with the other companies directly to share information and to shape the future development of the software.

Ways and Means

There are a myriad of IT products that have been explicitly developed to address some aspect of sustainability and many more products that though designed for more general purposes can be applied to sustainability-related objectives. The scale of these products ranges from ERP-like enterprise application suites to small apps that can be downloaded to a smartphone, and their cost ranges from hundreds of thousands of dollars to free. The challenge, therefore, is not in finding valuable means of partnering for sustainability, but rather it is to find ways to focus and prioritize the efforts to apply IT and to ensure that the various efforts come together in a synergistic whole.

To address the challenge we'll look at four ways to focus on a particular function within the organization:
- Focus on headquarters
- Focus on facilities and operations
- Focus on environmental health and safety
- Focus on product development and supply chain management

We'll also explore three ways of focusing on the enterprise as a whole:
- Focus on employees and teams
- Focus on the business model and its leverage points
- Focus on architecture

Focus on Headquarters

An essential responsibility of those who work in a corporate headquarters is to know what matters. With respect to sustainability, this means knowing the financially material costs and risks associated with the environmental impacts of current or proposed operations, the concerns of customers and rating agencies, and the likely return on investment for major internal sustainability initiatives that are underway or proposed. Partnering with the headquarters staff to help them meet their responsibilities is thus a great way to ensure that the IT sustainability program is focused on what matters. It is also, obviously, a high-leverage focus point because the decisions made at headquarters have wide-reaching impacts on the enterprise and its stakeholders.

In order to understand the ways and means of partnering with headquarters, it can be helpful to breakdown the requirements from the perspective of those who work there. The staff in a corporate or agency headquarters have three foci of concern with respect to sustainability that will benefit from effective IT support:

1. Information Needs of the Senior Leadership Team

A central focus in any headquarters is on the information needs of the senior leadership team, the CEO and his or her reports. As a result, a primary way of partnering with corporate staff is to provide them with the means to respond to queries from the leadership team for information or analysis and to provide regular reports on sustainability metrics. To do this effectively, you think through what information matters to the top executives by considering the sustainability-related challenges of their role as outlined in the following paragraphs.

Setting sustainability goals for the organization is a key responsibility of the leadership team and when they meet to do so, they will want to know information about current metrics, trends, and projections. They are likely to need information to answer questions such as: How much water do we use today? Has our usage been going up or down? If we set a goal for 10% reduction this year, can we meet it? Should we set goals for absolute reductions or should we normalize them against our billings? Are we confident enough of our goals to announce them publicly?

Tracking progress against goals is another key responsibility of leaders. Once goals are set, communicated to employees and the public, and perhaps even factored into executive bonus criteria, the leadership team will want to get timely progress reports and alerts of anything that is not on track and that needs more attention. When something shows up that is not on track, they will want to know what exactly is not on track and why and where and how to recover.

As the organization matures in setting and managing against sustainability goals, leadership may also begin to request not only information about the current situation and the past but also about the future. They may want to be kept abreast of projections such as what is the predicted unusually hot summer likely to do to our carbon footprint and how could we mitigate this? Or what will be the effect of winning a big new contract? And so on.

2. Performance Management of Functions and Business Units

A related area of focus of headquarter staff is the performance of internal functions and business units. "We're from corporate and we're here to help," is often said ironically, but in fact the only reason for having a corporate headquarters is to enable the various parts of the business to function. The functional executives in the corporate office need data that enables them to look across the company and see where things are going well so that they can recognize the people involved and so that they can help identify best practices that can be shared elsewhere. Perhaps more critically, they also need to be able to identify groups that are falling behind in meeting their goals so that help can be provided—the sooner that information indicating that problems are emerging, the sooner attention can be given and help provided.

Making investment decisions is another essential headquarters function and good sustainability-related information is needed to prioritize investments in sustainability improvements to ensure that money is focused on those opportunities that provide the greatest "bang for the buck" in terms of reducing carbon emissions, water use, or waste. In a large company or agency, it is likely that hundreds of investments in energy, water, and solid waste initiatives are made each year and done so with little insight into which promise the most environmental and financial return and even less insight into the returns that are actually achieved. Millions of dollars may be spent on these initiatives and the net return on investment on them can be improved greatly by improving the visibility executives have into how this money is being spent and the returns being achieved.

3. External Stakeholders

The third focus of headquarters we'll look at is communications with external stakeholders. The primary means of these communications, reporting, deserves special focus by the IT sustainability program because of its importance to the company and because of the opportunity it represents for IT to contribute. Helping the company to address its sustainability-related reporting requirements is a growing challenge affecting many parts of the company and, at the same time, supporting reporting is a well established role for IT. It is hard to imagine producing the quarterly financial reports in a large company today without IT support and in the future this will be the case for sustainability-related reporting as well. In any publicly traded company, the legally imposed reporting requirements are growing steadily and, at the same time, additional requirements are being driven by the expectations of investor groups and customers. The growth in requirements includes a growth in scope of data, the level of detail in the data, the frequency of data reporting, and the reliability of the data being reported.

A good way to understand the nature of these growing requirements is to look at the information challenges inherent in the framework for reporting carbon emissions—the GHG Protocol, which claims to be "the most widely used international accounting tool for government and business leaders to understand, quantify, and manage greenhouse gas emissions."[1] Most companies there have no legal requirement to report the data specified by the GHG Protocol, but the nonprofit Carbon Disclosure Project (CDP), which represents investors with assets totaling $41 trillion, regularly surveys large companies to assess investment-related risks and opportunities related to climate change using the Protocol as the framework. The size of the CDP's investment pool means that most large companies are responding to their survey or are preparing to do so in the future. In addition, these large companies are asking the smaller companies that are their suppliers to report their emissions. Since 2001, more than 1,000 businesses and organizations have developed their GHG inventories using the GHG

Protocol and anyone interested in applying IT for sustainability should have at least a high-level understanding of this framework.

The GHG Protocol covers the accounting and reporting of the six GHGs: carbon dioxide (CO_2), methane (CH_4), nitrous oxide (N_2O), hydrofluorocarbons (HFCs), perfluorocarbons (PFCs), and sulfur hexafluoride (SF_6). To help delineate direct and indirect emission sources and to provide utility for different types of organizations, three "scopes" (1, 2, and 3) are defined for GHG accounting and reporting purposes. The CDP requires that companies separately account for and report on scopes 1 and 2 at a minimum. The scopes are as follows:

- **Scope 1—Direct GHG emissions.** Direct GHG emissions occur from sources that are owned or controlled by the company. This includes, for example, emissions from the combustions associated with generators, boilers, furnaces, vehicles and the emissions from chemical production in owned or controlled process equipment.

- **Scope 2—Indirect GHG emissions.** Indirect GHG emissions result from the generation of electricity or by heating and cooling, or steam generated off-site but purchased by the company. For many companies, this is by far the largest component of their "carbon footprint."

- **Scope 3—Other indirect GHG emissions.** Scope 3 is an optional reporting category that allows for the treatment of all other indirect emissions that are a consequence of the activities of the company, but occur from sources not owned or controlled by the company. Some examples of Scope 3 emissions include employee travel and commuting, activities by vendors in the supply chain, and outsourced activities.

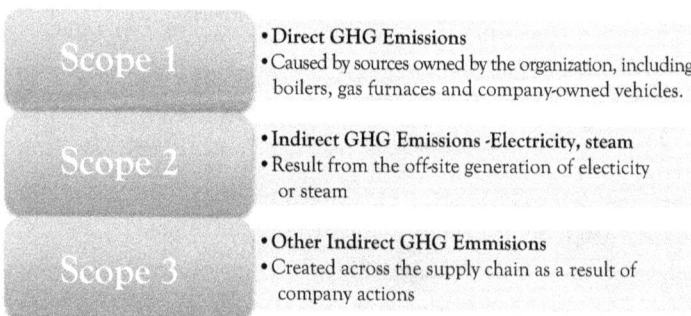

Scope 1	• Direct GHG Emissions • Caused by sources owned by the organization, including boilers, gas furnaces and company-owned vehicles.
Scope 2	• Indirect GHG Emissions ·Electricity, steam • Result from the off-site generation of electicity or steam
Scope 3	• Other Indirect GHG Emmisions • Created across the supply chain as a result of company actions

To understand the IT implications of GHG reporting, a good place to start is to consider Scope 2, which applies to all companies and agencies, whereas many nonmanufacturing, nonutility companies have little direct Scope 1 emissions, and Scope 3 emissions are optional and have not yet been addressed by a majority of companies. Conceptually, accounting for Scope 2 emissions seems simple enough—it's basically a reflection of how much electricity the company uses, and for small- or medium-sized companies that operate in just a few locations and pay just a few electricity bills each month, the reality is indeed fairly simple. They just need to collect the electricity usage from those bills each month and then apply the appropriate factor to determine how much GHGs were emitted to generate that electricity; this factor varies based on how the power was generated (e.g., natural gas versus different types of coal versus nuclear).

For large companies or agencies, however, this simple concept becomes quite challenging to implement. They have many sites in many locations, the bills go to many organizations in many divisions, the bills come at different times from different energy suppliers, the carbon factors for these suppliers vary by region and by supplier within a region, some sites are leased in agreements that hide the electricity bill, some sites lease space to others, and so on. Fortunately, the GHG Protocol provides a standard to report against so that it is possible for companies to use brute force in the form of manual entries from bills to spreadsheets, merging of spreadsheets, emails, reviews, re-reviews, and so forth, to compile the annual report of their Scope 2 emissions and most companies begin CHG this way.

However, while a largely manual method does meet the minimum requirements, there are important undesired effects related to cost, timeliness, and quality that suggest the value of a more robust IT solution. The cost effects arise from the "hidden factory" associated with the labor-intensive tasks of entering, compiling, and checking the data. Because these tasks are usually not anyone's "day job" they are often unaccounted for, but in a large company they can be significant when the total staff hours spent is considered. The timeliness issue is inherent in the fact that it takes an all out effort to produce a single report once in a year in time to meet the reporting deadline. While this "answers the mail," it does not provide data to manage progress throughout the year. Company management has no way of knowing whether the company is on track to meet GHG reduction goals set for the year, and site or business unit managers have no feedback on the results of any actions that they take to reduce energy use or on the impact of other actions that may be increasing energy use. The quality issue arises from the fact that lots of manual steps mean that there are lots of places for errors to be introduced and limited ways of catching those errors. In a large company, the use of manual methods also makes it difficult to support audits of the data, and this is becoming a concern as the visibility of GHG reporting data continues to grow and more companies seek third-party validation of their results, just as they do for financial reporting.

In response to the growing recognition of the challenge of GHGs and other forms of sustainability reporting, a vibrant market of IT solutions has emerged. In addition to participation by large established firms such as SAP, IBM, and CA, a number of startups including First Carbon Solutions, Manage CO2, Hara, C3, and many others now provide offerings focused specifically on this space. Because there are important advantages to doing so, most of these firms provide cloud-based solutions in addition to conventional internally hosted software packages. In addition to providing the normal cloud advantages of rapid implementation and lower operating costs, cloud-hosted sustainability reporting applications enable easier maintenance of the reference data that is needed to assess the location-dependent impact of electricity purchases or other activities. For example, most of the cloud-based solutions automatically incorporate updates from the EPA's eGRID (Emissions & Generation Resource Integrated Database) that provides data on the environmental characteristics of almost all electric power generated in the United States including the emissions for nitrogen oxides, sulfur dioxide, carbon dioxide, methane, and nitrous oxide. The cloud-based solutions also often offer extensive collections of integrations with utilities so that monthly usage information can be pulled in and combined with eGRID or other factors including weather information to rapidly provide updated information on footprint trends. Cloud-based solutions can also enable the collection of Scope 3 data that requires communications with supply chain partners. Whether cloud based or not solutions for sustainability reporting usually provide advanced reporting and analytical tools that provide visibility into the "hotspots" creating inordinate amounts of emissions, variances against trends that may indicate emerging problems, and predictions that can enable goal setting or early risk mediation efforts to ensure that previously set goals are accomplished. Another common feature is to provide reports organized and formatted for public reporting as specified by the CDP. A well-designed and maintained corporate sustainability information system can serve several business goals, including:

- Managing GHG emissions, water use, and other risks and identifying reduction opportunities
- Public reporting and participation in voluntary GHG reduction programs
- Participating in mandatory reporting programs
- Participating in GHG markets
- Recognition for voluntary action including tax credits or other local incentives

Focus on Facilities and Operations

The "Enterprise Smart Grid" is a term coined by Groom Energy[2] to refer to their vision of the systematic application of IT to the challenge of reducing the energy, water, and solid waste associated with operating the offices, factories, and other facilities of a company or agency. Other research firms are articulating similar visions and a growing number of IT suppliers are creating enterprise-scale IT systems and specialized point solutions that make the realization of these visions possible.

However, in many organizations there is a hidden barrier to realizing these visions—previous energy efficiency success. Most facilities organizations have been making steady progress on energy conservation for years, most buildings and factories are more energy efficient than they were in the past, and in most cases this has been accomplished without the aid of modern, enterprise-scale systems. Facilities engineers have been making do with spreadsheets, local databases, and disconnected building management systems while accomplishing steady year-over-year gains in energy efficiency. As a result, it is often effectively argued that there is no need for IT to engage with facilities and operations, as they have improvement processes that are working, so there is no need to spend money to improve them. "If it's not broken, don't fix it," as the saying goes.

Given this legitimate resistance, why should IT consider engaging with facilities and operations on energy use? What would be the basis for an initial dialogue? Several key points present themselves:

- **Buildings are where the energy use is.** For most organizations, the majority of GHG emissions and energy costs originate in buildings and the operations within them. Why do bank robbers rob banks? According to the U.S. Department of Energy, commercial buildings account for 19% of energy-related CO_2 emissions.[3]
- **The low-hanging fruit has been picked.** Most facilities teams have already done a great job of replacing lighting fixtures, replacing old HVAC gear, fixing air leaks that are visible, and working through the actions identified in energy audits. How will facilities continue to provide the annual cost savings to which management has become accustomed?
- **Data overwhelm is growing.** More and more of the new components in buildings have sensors, are connected to the network, and send out status reports every 15 minutes. Also, more submeters are being installed that have similar Gatling gun like data characteristics. This data has the potential to become great information, but who has time to look at it all? How does anybody make sense of it?
- **Success stories are emerging.** New information technologies that support this sector are maturing and are being implemented with dramatic success. As with other parts of the enterprise, leveraging the latest technology is often essential to remain competitive.

To further motivate exploration of an IT engagement with facilities and operations, we'll look first at the limitations of some of the common current state information sources and then visit the story of the "building whisperer" at IBM and how he engaged with the facilities team there that already had a great record of energy improvements and were thus understandably skeptical of his initial advances.

The Limitations of Power Bills and Audits

While compiling the utility bills from across the company is an adequate means to calculate the impact of GHGs on operating its facilities and is a necessary and nontrivial task, it is not a sufficient basis for optimal energy management. This can be seen by comparison to an information source many of us rely on in our personal lives—cell phone bills. When we receive our family cell phone bill, we can see a breakdown of just how we spent our minutes, which numbers were called, from which numbers, at what time of the day, and for how long. In the case of long calls, we are likely to remember the occasion because it occurred just in the last month. If we were charged at a higher rate for calls during business hours, we'll be able to see that and any calls at highly discounted rates will be visible as well. With this information, we can identify patterns or usage habits that we can change in order to reduce our bills, and then, in subsequent months, we'll be able to track the extent to which we did in fact change our habits and the changes resulted in reducing our bills.

In contrast, the monthly electricity bill for a facility is likely to only provide information about the amount due and the total number of kilowatt-hours used that month. From that information, an energy manager can determine if more or less energy was used than in the previous month, or than in the same month in the previous year, but the bill will provide no clues as to why the energy use was high or low. If the bill is reviewed in a time period close to the month in which the charges occurred, the manager may be able to rationalize how the weather drove the bill one or the other way or compare the bill for one site against another of a similar size in a similar location; but the reality is that the bill provides very little actionable information. Managing energy with monthly bills as the only information source is like managing cash flow with only the end of month totals. The situation can be even worse for an energy manager responsible for several locations who doesn't even get the monthly bills for all of his or her sites until several months have passed.

In order to develop strategies to reduce the energy spent at a facility, the energy manager requires information such as:

- Timing of the energy use—the breakdown of energy use by time of day and day of the month
- Location of the energy use—how much is coming from office space, from the factory floor, or from the on-site computer room
- Correlations—how does the energy usage track against outside air temperatures, holidays, changes to the facility, or factory production levels

- Unexpected discrepancies—the energy use in Wing B rose significantly starting on the 14th, but the other wings did not see increased energy use

Armed with such information, an energy manager is much better able to identify opportunities for improvement and then to validate the impact of improvements when they are made. For example, if the energy use is not dipping as much as expected on weekends or holidays, perhaps automated lighting timers can be installed or temperature setbacks programmed; or if a large percentage of the site's energy is being used in the computer room, facilities can be instructed to team with IT to see what can be done; and noticing unexpected changes in Wing B's energy use can lead to the discovery that its air conditioning hardware is starting to fail.

The Building Whisperer

"Listening to Buildings"[4] is the title of talk given by IBM vice president Dave Bartlett where he tells the story of how after first gaining the backing of his CEO he persuaded the company's facilities teams to let him apply IBM's data capture and data analytics technologies to their buildings in support of achieving greater energy use reductions. As Bartlett tells the story, the facilities folks were quite skeptical of the IT guy who showed up at their door. They already had a mature energy program that was producing 6% reduction in energy use each year and it was hard for them to see how a guy from IT who did not know their business was going to do anything but get in their way and spend company money. However, he had the direct support of the CEO, so they proceeded anyway at a selected set of large campuses and the results turned them from being skeptics to becoming advocates. The application of IT led to achieving 8% reduction on top of their previous 6% and achieving a 200% return on investment.

Bartlett does not mention product names, but he does describe the main elements of the IT solution that produced these dramatic results and helped him become a self-described "building whisperer" able to listen to buildings and hear what they were saying about why and where they were using excessive amounts of energy. The first element was to connect the thousands of sensors now provided by equipment makers such as Siemens and Johnson Controls in the smart equipment they now make that are distributed across company campuses—refrigerators, air conditioners, air movers, lighting systems, water heaters, computer rooms, projectors, elevators, and so on. "There's a huge proliferation of smart sensor technology where we can see—with much better x-ray vision—what's happening with our building, with our transport system, with our energy networks."[5] To gain access to this data, IBM used IP networking (extending their existing local area networks or LANs) to enable the data being produced by these sensors to be transmitted and captured in a central location.

Of course, thousands of sensors sending readings every 15 minutes are going to produce a huge amount of data that could quickly become not only a storage problem but also unintelligible, so IBM had to use it experience with storage, databases, data warehouses, analytics, and rule engines to create the other part of the solution. They also worked closely with the experts in facilities to identify the most important sensors to read and to build up the rule bases that would help them to understand and respond to what the sensors (a.k.a. the buildings) were telling them. When the combined power of sensors, network, data management, and analytics is integrated, site managers can "listen" holistically to their buildings in a way that is simply not possible by looking at the output of smart devices one at a time. A powerful example of the benefit of doing this is that they often identify cases where disconnected, low-level automation is leading to air conditioners cooling air at the same time as other equipment in the building is heating it. The environment also allows staff to identify and respond to issues in near real time and perform maintenance before energy- or water-wasting degradation occurs in systems.

This information environment also enables the company to prioritize investments in equipment upgrades and to then track the benefits that result from the investment, which builds their learning and greatly helps to justify future investments. This ability to target, justify, and track investments is by itself a breakthrough capability. While it is well known that energy or water savings investments tend to pay for themselves, facilities departments the world over are hamstrung by a lack of data when it comes to being able to make the business case for a particular investment because they are unable to say with authority why that is the best opportunity for investment in energy or water savings and because they don't have the historic or analytic data to predict exactly what the payback time will be. The data provided by environments such as that mentioned in the IBM example also allow companies to be more aggressive in setting goals for carbon footprint or water use reduction because they have insight into the leverage points they have to work with and don't have to rely on simply committing to working hard at it.

The bottom line for IBM is that from 2008 to 2011, as they rolled out this approach across their sites worldwide, they "saved over $50 million in electricity expenses and conserved 523,000 megawatt hours of electricity ... enough to power 47,000 average U.S. homes for a year."[6] "No one is listening holistically to buildings," Bartlett says. "There's automation device by device, or system by system, but no one is watching the sum of the systems, and doing so can deliver savings of 40% or more." In addition to providing operational savings, this internal experience provided the learning and confidence the company needed to launch a line of "Smart Building" products and services offerings. The bottom line for IT sustainability programs is that they have the opportunity to help their facilities partners become "building whisperers."

Overcoming Technical Barriers

Once the cultural barrier to fully leveraging information for energy efficiency has been overcome and energy managers see the potential value of partnering with IT, two more technical barriers will likely present themselves. The first and most fundamental challenge is that the means to capture the needed data may not be in place. If the electricity meter for the facility is simply an old-fashioned set of dials, the only way to get information from it is to manually go and read it, meaning that it is likely to be impractical to get more than a monthly reading. Also, if the only meter for the facility is at the electrical front door, no means will be available to see where the energy is flowing within the buildings.

Fortunately, affordable means of meeting the challenge of providing energy use information are rapidly becoming available. For example, more and more utilities offer their customers "smart meters" that provide "interval" energy use data in electronic form. With such a meter, it is possible to record the energy use every 15 minutes and send that information to a database anywhere in the world. New means of obtaining visibility into where the energy goes within a facility are also becoming available. Submeters, which can be installed to capture the energy flowing into a particular part of the facility, have long been available but are now also becoming smarter. Though they can still be expensive to install, their electronics now makes getting data from them much more affordable.

In addition to meters, innovative means are emerging that make timely data capture more granular and affordable. Just about all new equipment installed in a facility today is likely to have embedded sensors (this is a true megatrend) and have the means to be assigned an IP address. Refrigeration units, pumps, motors, fans, lighting, and so on are increasing able to provide information to the network on their energy use, temperature, and other variables every few minutes. To exploit this data, companies like Joule-X and its competitors are providing software-based means of collecting this information. Their software data can pull in data from any device with an IP address or from older equipment that can be front-ended with a network connector. In addition, the energy use of older equipment that cannot be networked can be modeled by referring to their specifications or by one-time metering; these models are used in real time to yield actual information that provides a detailed understanding of where energy is used in a facility.

The second big challenge to providing facilities managers with the information they need to optimize energy use can be understood by contemplating the volume of data implied by the above discussion on networked meters and sensors. A campus with hundreds or even thousands of components sending out updates every 15 minutes will within an hour create more information than anyone will be able to make use of without a supporting system. We might use the term "information overload" to describe this situation, but "data overload" might be a more accurate term. An overwhelming amount of data actually is not in itself useful information and may be a barrier to perceiving useful information about the environment if the means to makes sense of it all are not provided.

Fortunately, IT systems are available for just this task. Managing the large volumes of data and processing and presenting energy managers and site owners with useful information about the patterns of energy use can now be supported by systems that help collect the data, provide a means to analyze it, provide automatic alerts, and provide automated control to continuously optimize operations. The U.S. EPA's cloud-based Energy Star Portfolio Manager,[7] for example, is "an interactive energy management tool that allows you to track and assess energy and water consumption across your entire portfolio of buildings in a secure online environment. Whether you own, manage, or hold properties for investment, Portfolio Manager can help you set investment priorities, identify under-performing buildings, verify efficiency improvements, and receive EPA recognition for superior energy performance."

In addition, commercial software providers including SAP, CA, Joule-X, Schneider, C3, Hara and a growing list of others are using enterprise class databases, analytical engines, reporting tools, and portal interfaces to enable making sense from the vast quantities of data now available. They enable facilities managers to see trends and patterns that indicate problems such as an equipment that is degrading, spot opportunities such as adjusting a building's systems so that heating and cooling systems are not automatically responding to each other and working at the same time; to prioritize investment opportunities by using data to see where the biggest returns can be realized; and to monitor the results of improvements that are made. Rather than relying on a yearly audit to identify the problems that can be seen in a facility, facilities staff can now make continuous improvements throughout the year based on what can be seen and what is unseen using the combination of data and information management systems that is now available.

Focus on Environmental Health and Safety

The environmental health and safety (EHS) function plays a key role in sustainability in most companies and agencies. In many cases, however, they fall behind finance or supply chain or engineering in terms of getting IT support and have a long-standing need for better IT systems to manage their complex reporting requirements on everything from worker safety and ergonomics to hazardous waste handling and site-remediation efforts. EHS staff may also be responsible for putting together reports on sustainability metrics such as GHG emissions and water usage and may be doing so via a painstaking application of multiple spreadsheets and homegrown databases.

A focus on headquarters along the lines discussed earlier will help EHS to increase the productivity and quality of the sustainability reporting process. Beyond this, however, it is also valuable to focus on EHS as a function, partnering with them to leverage IT for the full range of services they provide, all of which contribute to sustainability in some way. In this book, we've focused on environmental sustainability, but the health and safety of employees is part of the full, "triple-bottom-line," view of sustainability. Working with EHS to deploy an integrated platform that meets the need of their employees and their customers is a high-leverage way to address both people and planet sustainability issues. It is also likely to be a way to increase profits, by reducing the labor of both EHS staff and other employees and by retiring many of the point-solution systems that have been implemented in most large organizations. Effective software for providing an integrated EHS platform is available from broad-based business software companies like SAP, and from a number of firms that specialize in EHS and sustainability like Enablon and IHS.

When selecting the supplier, a primary criterion should be how their products contribute to the full architecture of IT for sustainability solutions in the company. A potential for confusion or misstep exists here because of the likely overlap of functionality with applications that support the corporate staff in managing key sustainability metrics (e.g., carbon emissions and water use) or with applications used by facilities to optimize energy use. A key way of addressing this issue when selecting the EHS system is to make a conscious decision about the extent to which it should also provide the basis for meeting the needs of headquarters for sustainability governance and reporting. Some of the product offerings for EHS are quite capable of supporting this larger role, while others have significant limitations. For example, they may provide limited carbon reporting, but fall short of providing a basis for complete Scope 1, 2, and 3 carbon emissions or lack the means to effectively gather and integrate information from utilities. Systems with such limitations can still be good choices for EHS if they are designed so that they can be integrated into a larger systems environment. Similar thought should be given to how the EHS system functionality will fit with systems used by other functions, especially those used by facilities for energy and water use optimization. The EHS platforms tend to have a "module for everything," but in some cases these will fall significantly short of meeting specialized needs in certain areas.

Focus on Product Development and Supply Chain Management

The biggest sustainability lever for companies that sell manufactured products is likely to be the design of the products themselves. A car company, for example, can make a bigger impact on the environment by changing the design of its cars than by optimizing the energy use in its factories and offices. The design, most obviously, will affect how much fuel is used by its cars over their useful lives and, less obviously, will also determine how much energy, water, and other resources are needed in the manufacture of the car and the extent to which the car can be recycled at the end of its life. As a result, leading companies are very focused on product sustainability and there are several important ways that IT can partner with engineering to embed sustainability concerns into product development and thereby create products that are more sustainable:

- **Support life cycle analysis.** IT systems can provide data and analytics that enable product designers to reduce the amount of energy, carbon, and water required to source and produce a product. The more that IT can put this information at the fingertips of designers, the more they can use it as a basis of design choices. The information developed by this analysis can also be provided to customers as part of the value proposition for the product.

- **Provide modeling and simulation.** These powerful tools are key to designing products that use fewer resources to manufacture and to operate. They can also reduce the need for building and testing physical prototypes.

- **Enable tracking materials of concern.** IT systems can enable tracking and reducing the use of materials of concern such as heavy metals, conflict minerals, hazardous chemicals, and other similar materials in design. Especially for assemblies with large bills of materials, IT systems are essential for this task. They can import bill of material data to quickly highlight critical components and generate the reporting required by regulations.

The other key function, along with engineering, in the product life cycle is supply chain management (SCM). SCM has long depended on IT to operate successfully and now leading companies are extending this relationship to further sustainability goals. This can include providing information to employees regarding supply chain choices, optimizing the routing of supplies to minimize energy use and other environmental impacts, and systems support for managing and reporting on Scope 3 GHG emissions. The Scope 3 standard, which was developed as the result of a 3-year multi-stakeholder process, includes both requirements and guidance for the expanded scope that goes well beyond a company's direct emissions from facilities and vehicles (Scope 1), and purchased energy for their infrastructure (Scope 2), to include purchased goods and services, transportation and distribution, use of sold products, end-of-life product management, business travel, waste, investments, and other areas encompassing both upstream and downstream activities. Scope 3 will likely be the area where most companies will find both the largest opportunities for emissions reductions and the most difficulty in tracking them—hence the opportunity for IT to contribute!

The supply chain footprint can be broken down into three areas: movement, space, and material. Movement includes total inbound shipment of raw materials and parts, movement of material from work in progress to finished goods. It also includes total outbound shipments into the distribution network as well as reverse logistics for any product returns from customers. Space includes warehousing, trailer yards, and factory space. Materials include the component materials of the product, waste streams, and the product at end-of-life. Each element of this supply chain provides a potential leverage point for reducing the overall environmental impact of the enterprise. In addition to supporting metrics reporting, IT can help product developers to perform a life cycle assessment (LCA) that assesses the total environmental impact of producing, delivering, and retiring a particular product.

Focus on Employees and Teams

In addition to supporting particular functions as described above, there are many ways in which IT can support individual employees and teams regardless of their role in the organization. This is a particularly dynamic area of IT development and so the discussion that follows is intended not

Table 4.1. Possible Leverage Points in the Supply Chain.

	Inbound	Production	Distribution	Reverse logistics
Movements	Total inbound shipments by air, truck and ocean	movements from raw material to work in progress to finished goods	Total outbound shipments in the distribution network	Total returns from the customers
Space	Traileryard, raw material warehouse space	Factory space, traileryard	Warehouse Space, trailer yard, fleet	Warehouse space
Material	Supplier production process, weight of raw material	Process time, material yield rate	Weight of product	Process of refurbishment, process of obsolesce waste management

to be definitive, but rather to be suggestive of new means that are emerging almost daily.

1. Reduce Business Travel

Reducing business travel is a way to significantly reduce the indirect (i.e., "Scope 3") carbon emissions of any organization and for some, such as professional services firms, it will be the highest leverage way of doing so. Reducing travel will also reduce expenses, free up staff time, and enhance work–life balances, so it is clearly a good domain for IT focus. A caution, however, is that these benefits must always be weighed against the value that does come from travel, such as seeing customers face to face and enabling creative work by teams.

The most obvious means for reducing travel are alternatives to in-person meetings such as video teleconferencing (VTC) and web-based meeting services that allow remote screen sharing. These technologies have been around for some time and are present in most large organizations, but adding a new focus to them may be merited because of ongoing enhancements to the technologies and because there are nontechnical means by which IT can increase the value that the organization receives by using them.

Telepresence is a term used to describe what is essentially a high-end version of VTC. Providers such as Cisco and HP make use of high definition cameras, screens, microphones, and speakers along with special networking and specially designed rooms to provide an experience that is much closer to "face to face" than conventional VTC, even giving participants the feeling that they are actually present with each other. The following set of features listed on Cisco's website to describe one of their products is illustrative the technology being used:

- Three 65-inch screens are positioned to reduce camera intrusion while maintaining eye gaze.
- A state-of-the-art, three-camera cluster allows for greater eye contact and a continuous whole-room experience with no field-of-view overlap.
- Uniquely designed, one-inch thin light reflector provides integrated lighting with reduced glare; light reflector can be wall-mounted or freestanding.
- Integrated microphones provide better frequency pickup and shielding to block mobile and wireless device interference.

While the use of such components is expensive, they can be cost effective when compared with cost savings from a percentage of executive travel costs.

A lower cost way in which VTC technology is evolving is through increasingly affordable means to conference using personal computers and mobile devices in the corporate environment. Employees and teams can now operate securely in the work environment in much the same way that many of them do in their personal lives using Skype over the Internet. With or without video, web-based meeting services such as WebEx and GoToMeeting and internally hosted services such as IBM's Sametime provide a low-cost, per-meeting service that enables much of the presenting, demonstrating, and screen-based collaborating that are large components of many meetings.

In addition to providing technologies such as those described above, IT can add value by finding ways to make virtual meetings more effective. For example, they can develop and promulgate best practices for facilitating or participating in remote meetings, ensure that conference rooms are well provisioned, and make it easy to sign up online to use special telepresence rooms while retaining the prerogatives of executives to use them when they need them.

Databases and applications are other less obvious means of reducing travel. SAP, for example, significantly reduced the amount of travel by its consultants by developing an application that enabled managers to first check if consultants with needed skills were already located in a region rather than simply sending folks from one part of the continent to another based just on expertise.[8] Other data-driven means of reducing travel include metrics dashboards that show progress against travel reduction goals and the resulting environmental and financial savings, and data from travel services that enable those booking travel to make choices informed by the carbon footprint of various options.

2. Reduce Commuting and Office Space

IT, working with HR and facilities, can also help employees reduce the environmental impact of commuting. Ways to do this include providing a database that allows employees to coordinate ride sharing, promoting the use of websites that allow employees to select mass transit options, provisioning virtual private networks that allow employees to telecommute, and providing applications that help facilities to implement "hoteling" office approaches, where employees who telecommute a portion of their week use an application to reserve office space just when needed. It is important to note that, in addition to reducing travel, supporting hoteling also allows facilities to reduce their total floor space requirements and the associated environmental footprints of their buildings while saving money.

3. Provide a Social Networking Platform

One of most significant leverage points for any organization's sustainability efforts is the social capital of its workforce. Idea generation and implementation of ideas are both paced by relationships and informal knowledge sharing processes and IT can increase the strength of the functions by providing an internal platform for social networking. The potential for this can be seen by looking at the impact of internet sites like Facebook and Twitter—they have famously supported major social movements that were reported in the news and also support the quiet growth of hundreds of thousands of communities each day.

Unfortunately, however, the utility of using these sites to support communities that are internal to a company is limited by privacy concerns. Even an organization that is committed to transparency is likely to want to protect the ability of its employees to have private discussions about sensitive issues and to protect its intellectual property from competitors. As a result, many companies are provisioning internal social platforms using products such as IBM's Connections, SocialText, or knitting together combinations of tools including wikis, portals, and collaboration tools to create a custom platform.

Of course, in most cases when companies or agencies choose to invest in such platforms, they do so for broader reasons than just supporting the sustainability program. The sustainability program can do a great deal, however, to maximize the value received from these investments by fostering sustainability-related communities, wikis, blogs, discussions, and so on. The IT sustainability program in particular has the opportunity to be a leader in this and doing so will not only help sustainability efforts, but will also help IT to succeed in gaining adoption of the social platform.

4. Provide Employee- or Team-Specific Information

The "Prius effect" refers to the change in driving habits of Prius drivers that comes from the real-time information provided to them on the dashboard about how efficiently they are driving, not only at the end of a tank of gas, but in real time. Because they are able, moment by moment, to see the extent to which they are using the battery and gasoline leads, they tend to ease out of stoplights, coast when they can, and think twice before increasing their speed.

An ideal way of engaging employees in sustainability would be to provide them with the Prius-like means of seeing the impact of their actions throughout the day in terms of water, energy, and solid waste. In many cases, this by itself would lead to employees striving to minimize their footprint and maximize positive metrics. And for those with a competitive streak, this dynamic would be intensified if they could compare and compete based on these numbers.

The challenge, however, is that for most jobs providing feedback on the environmental impact of workplace actions is not as simple as it is in the well-bounded situation of driving a car. If you turn off the headlights in a Prius you'll see a slight change in battery usage, but if you turn off the lights in your office it's unlikely that there is data available to show you the impact of that in real time, or even to do so at the end of the month.

In order to get around this data-gap challenge, we may have to be willing to accept one or more forms of imprecision in the data that we provide. One form of doing this is to use data for a larger unit of which the individual employee is a part. For example, feedback on facility-related sustainability actions such as reducing energy or water use or minimizing solid waste can often be provided at the site level and perhaps even at the level of a floor or building module. Extracting this data from the databases where it resides and making it available in a user-friendly, granular manner and as close to real time as possible will empower employees to make more sustainable choices in their workdays. In addition, providing the information about how local efforts compare with that of other localities enables competitive juices to be engaged.

Another form of imprecision that may useful to accept in order to provide still-valuable feedback is to use data based on estimates or norms. For example, estimates of the carbon used for a typical car driving to work versus that used by typical mass transit systems are used by internet-based applications that allow individuals to track their personal carbon footprints. Estimates can also be very useful in providing feedback on work-related processes and products. For example, estimates based on studies of the carbon impact of truck loading percentage can be used to provide information to a shipping company employee about the carbon generated per ton-mile of cargo.

Focus on the Business Model and Its Leverage Points

A key element of sustainability strategy is to identify and exploit the leverage points that are unique to an organization. Walmart, for example, has famously focused on using its tremendous market presence to drive sustainability reporting requirements onto those who want to sell in their stores and to reduce the waste in packaging. UPS, on the other hand, has focused on making its deliveries as energy efficient as possible and on providing its customers with information on the carbon impact of individual shipments.

So far we've addressed finding ways to partner on sustainability with other corporate functions on processes that are common to most companies, but we now turn to partnering in ways that are specific to your company's business model. Here the idea is to look at the ways that are distinctive about the value proposition that the company offers to customers or that drive a large portion of the company's environmental footprint in search of ways to innovate in applying IT to increase customer value or reduce operating costs while also enhancing environmental sustainability.

There is necessarily no formula for doing this, as the business model, the functions IT partners with, and the applications used will be different. The one constant for IT staff is that they need to proactively think about the company's business model and reach out to functions to have these discussions. For leaders across the business, the constant is to ask the question about how sustainability-related innovation might make their domains more competitive and to reach back to IT for their help in making it happen. In lieu of a formula, then, the following are examples from several industries that are illustrative of the opportunity to build competitive advantage by making a distinctive contribution to global sustainability.

Clothing and Consumer Goods

Consumer goods manufacturers are increasingly being driven by the preferences of their end customers to compete on the basis of the sustainability or "greenness" of their products and companies. In addition, retailers such as Walmart are compelling them to provide information about the life cycle footprints of their products and to show progress in reducing these footprints. As a result, industry leaders are developing innovative IT solutions that give them a leg up with consumers or that help them to meet the requirements of retailers for sustainability information in a cost-effective manner. Illustrative examples include:

- **Patagonia** is a clothing and outdoors gear company for whom environmental responsibility is a primary component of their brand and they support this through an innovative application of IT on their website. For example a feature called "The Footprint Chronicles (Registered)," "examines Patagonia's life and habits as a company," with the goal of using "transparency about our supply chain to help us reduce our adverse social and environmental impacts – and on an industrial scale enables customers and the public at large to view a detailed life cycle analysis of the footprint of each of their products including the ability to move graphically through the supply chain."[9]

- **Unilever** has an interactive application on its website called the "Product Analyzer" that allows anyone to select any of its 1,600 products and then view the water, waste, or GHG footprint for that product. Importantly, the footprint is shown not only for the raw materials, manufacture, and distribution of the product but also for its use so that the public is educated about how Unilever has identified that a key sustainability leverage point for their company is to reduce the energy, water, and waste associated with the use of its products such as detergents, soaps, and food products.[10]

- **Nike** has an initiative that asks apparel designers and developers to use sustainable materials listed in the Nike Materials Sustainability Index and to build a new database about their suppliers. The goal is for shoe and clothing makers worldwide to select materials based on sustainability, comparing, for example, organic cotton from an average supplier to nonorganic cotton from a better supplier, and being able to figure out quickly which is better.[11]

Cities and Regional Governments

Cities and other regional governments compete for reputation, business relocations, and residents and, increasingly, this competition is being extended to the area of sustainability. For example, Phoenix Mayor Greg Stanton's stated bluntly, "Leading in Sustainability is not easy; however, as mayor, I am committed to doing so."[12] The planet is estimated to have 9 billion people by 2050, and much of that growth will happen in urban areas. Traffic congestion, air pollution, crime, and general inefficiency are among a host of problems that plague growing cities and that, data suggest, actually grow at a faster rate than the cities themselves. Examples of creative responses to these challenges by cities and regional governments include the following:

- **The Hestia system**[13] is being used in urban areas to "identify CO_2 emission sources in a way that policy makers can utilize and the public can understand." Just as enterprise sustainability management systems can help companies identify the most beneficial places to make energy or water saving investments, the Hestia system developed at Arizona State University enables cities to identify the best place to make an investment in GHG reduction. According to ASU professor Kevin Gurney, "with Hestia, we can provide cities with a complete, three-dimensional picture of where, when and how carbon dioxide emissions are occurring." The system is loaded with data from sources such as air pollution reports, traffic counts, and tax assessor information and then this data is combined with "a modeling system for quantifying CO_2 emissions at the level of individual buildings and street segments." This precise yet comprehensive information will help city officials identify where best to make investments to reduce energy use and GHG emissions.

- **Intelligent transportation systems (ITS)** can "make traffic flow more smoothly by controlling traffic lights to match changing conditions, advising drivers about hazards or jams ahead, using ramp meters to smoothly insert autos into traffic, or charging tolls on the fly electronically, to name just a few."[14] In addition to reducing carbon emissions, taking these steps reduces fuel expenses and time wasted by citizens in traffic.

- **Sewage is being managed like traffic.** South Bend, Indiana, is using a sensor network, big data, and analytic software to prevent its sewer system from dumping sewage into rivers or backing up into citizens' homes.[15]

- **Parking systems** such as that being deployed in Los Angles can relieve traffic congestion, reduce air pollution, and carbon emissions by implementing demand-based pricing that adjusts parking rates based on driver demand for spaces and availability.[16] By increasing rates in high demand spots, there is the potential for more parking spaces to become available in each block—reducing traffic congestion and pollution generated by drivers hunting for curbside parking. It may also encourage drivers to consider carpooling, bicycling, and public transportation as alternatives.

Franchise and Real Estate Management

Many real estate companies, retailers, and restaurant chains manage a portfolio of properties in many locations across the country (or countries). Energy costs can be an important component of operating costs for these organizations and sustainability performance is likely to be of increasing importance to customers. The highly distributed nature of the resources involved in this situation mean that collecting and distributing information is a challenge to effective IT support. It also means that the labor and travel expenses of manually performing audits of energy or water can be prohibitive. Other common challenges include gaining access to needed information when leasing space in larger facilities and the special metrics associated with the particular chain or industry such as the cost of refrigeration or amount of food waste.

In response to these challenges, a number of cloud-based IT solutions are emerging that target sustainability management for these industries. The cloud-based approach is a great fit for this market because it addresses the problem of collecting data and distributing results. It also helps the provider to rapidly incorporate changes to functionality or configurations as required by businesses that must always be dynamically responding to their customers. Examples of sustainability management solutions being applied in this space include:

- **Starbucks** piloted the use of the cloud-based Building Dashboard service provided by Lucid with the intent of enabling store employees to enact energy saving practices while not hurting customer service.[17]
- **Cox Enterprises** is using a service from Urjanet to collect its electricity use information from the 190 utilities that provide power to its distributed operations. Cox "used the data to eliminate assets that they were paying for but no longer using and moving some of its 30,000 utility accounts to alternate rates that saved money for customers."[18]
- **Virtual energy audits** provided by several new companies allow holders of large portfolios to use monthly utility data combined with information about weather, location, building function, and so on to provide screening audits that highlight which properties merit further attention.

Shipping and Logistics

Increasingly sustainability is a basis of competitive advantage for shipping and logistics organizations. Customers ranging from individual consumers to the largest retailers and manufacturers increasingly are considering factors such as the carbon footprint of making a shipment when deciding which shipper to select. In addition, companies (and government organizations such as the military) for whom logistics is a major component of their operations are finding that focusing on sustainability in this domain can be a means of significant environmental and financial returns.

Information technology can make a big contribution to reducing the carbon emissions associated with shipping by enabling firms to optimize how trucks are packed and routed. A large truck, for example, produces half as much CO_2 per ton-mile when it is fully packed as opposed to when it is 65% full[19] and fleet owners can use algorithms to consolidate shipments and reduce the carbon per ton-mile. Route selection can also be improved to reduce distance traveled, avoid congestion, and, as in the technique made famous by FedEx, avoid left turns. UPS has implemented several tools and procedures, called Package Flow Technologies, to optimize delivery routes. Since 2001, UPS has optimized its processes of allocating pickups and deliveries to the most efficient number of vehicles and has avoided driving 183 million miles, resulting in reduced fuel use and less emissions.[20] UPS Airlines uses a special program to calculate the most efficient routes based on weather, winds, terrain, and other factors, and through various strategies, including the redispatch of international flights, the program has managed to save more than one million gallons of fuel. IT solutions can also enable the use of lower impact means of shipping such as rail and reduce the need for the use of air transport. When combined, these techniques can make a material reduction in both the environmental and financial costs of shipping.

Another way that shippers are using IT to enhance sustainability is by providing information to their customers about the amount of carbon emissions associated with various shipment options so that they can make better choices as part of optimizing the footprint of their overall operations and so that they can more easily track their Scope 3 emissions. IT also enables firms such as FedEx and UPS to offer carbon neutral shipping options to their customers.

Travel Industry

The travel industry is making extensive use of IT to provide information to customers about their travel choices. From the travel agent to the airline or ground transport provider, to the hotel, leading providers are providing information about carbon emissions to their corporate and individual customers who increasingly make purchase selections based on the ability to have access to this information and on the comparisons between options.

Utilities

With the advent of the so-called Smart Grid, the electrical utility industry is becoming IT intensive. IT control systems, big data analytics, and cyber security are absolutely essential to the vision of using high levels of renewable energy sources because they are more distributed and have more variable power output as compared with conventional sources requiring sophisticated means of balancing supply and demand. IT systems are also essential to providing utility customers with the information they need to bring down their usage and costs. Due to the high volumes of data (thousands of locations on the grid reporting every few minutes), the need for real-time solutions, and the cyber security threat, the application of IT for utilities and the grid is pushing the state of the art and is an interesting book-length topic in itself. For an introduction to this rapidly emerging field, the reader is referred to the relevant chapters in Armory Lovins' important book *Reinventing Fire: Bold Business Solutions for the New Energy Era.*[21]

New Business Models

IT can enable new business models that are explicitly focused on providing innovative services for consumer or business customers who are concerned about sustainability. Innovative use of IT in this area can be the basis for launching new companies, new businesses within existing companies, or new services within government agencies. Suggestive examples include:

- **Zipcar** is "redefining what green looks like" using an innovative suite of information technologies including RFID, smartphone applications, and analytics to enable car sharing for both consumers and businesses. They believe that each of their shared cars takes

20 other cars off the roads and that they enable their members to drive less miles per year saving 219 gallons per Zipster (customer) according to their website.

- **Recycle Bank** makes innovative use of IT to support its mission "to realize a world where nothing is wasted." Individuals can earn points for adopting green behaviors and then use those points to get rewards. Cities and companies, meanwhile, partner with Recycle Bank to promote community-specific behaviors or their brand, products, and services.

- **AngelPoints** uses IT to provide an integrated platform that provides the tools companies need to drive programs that change the way their employees and customers perceive them. According to their website, they "give you the technology you need to rally employees, encouraging them to be more involved with your volunteering, giving, and sustainability programs. And we allow you to gain efficiencies and utilize fewer resources in the process, ultimately saving you time and money and allowing you to make a greater difference."

- **ParkatmyHouse.com** provides a web-based service that allows people to rent out their private parking spaces to drivers. By using the service, would-be parkers avoid overpriced, scarce parking on streets or in parking lots and greatly reduce the energy use in a city associated with drivers circling to find a parking space.

Focus on Architecture

So far we've focused on the discrete chunks of functionality of IT for sustainability, but as we've seen it's perhaps obvious that there are significant overlaps and a real need for interconnectedness. For example, the detailed data used by an energy engineer optimizing the cooling of a facility is connected, ultimately, with the information in the GHG report that the corporate offices produce. In order to create such connections, an IT for sustainability architecture is needed that not only provides discrete sets of functionality, but that also supports the enterprise in developing a holistic approach to sustainability. In a healthy company, the corporate office staff and the employees in the field feel themselves to be working together on the same challenges and in a company that is a sustainability leader, sustainability is not a standalone effort, but is embedded in all strategies and practices. IT architecture should contribute to this connectedness rather than detract from it.

An important way, therefore, for the IT sustainability program to further the company's sustainability efforts is to work with enterprise architects to ensure that the set of systems employed form a coherent whole in which conceptual integrity is maintained across systems and that needed integrations are provided between them. It is also important to ensure that the sustainability environment is integrated with the larger IT architecture, including enterprise resource planning, SCM, product life cycle management, and customer relationship management systems, so that sustainability can be integral to finance, supply chain, engineering, and other business processes.

One potential means of achieving this integration is through the suppliers of your sustainability applications. Many of these firms provide integrated suites of systems and also provide integrations of their software to popular business systems. The clear implication here is that the ability of a potential supplier to provide integration and contribute to a holistic environment should be an important criterion when selecting software systems for sustainability. Also, you should seek to fully leverage the product lines and intellectual property of the suppliers that you do select. Your enterprise architecture function will be aware of additional means of integration that are supported within the enterprise.

Summary

Trends

- **"Green IT 2.0."** Both industry analysts and practitioners are recognizing that the scope of IT sustainability or "green IT" must extend beyond a focus on IT operations to address the larger footprint of the company or agency.
- **Stakeholder expectations are rising.** The expectations of external stakeholders for information about the sustainability performance of organizations and the life cycle impact of products and services continues to grow steadily. Also growing is the expectation for improved sustainability performance.

- **"There's an app for that."** Sustainability efforts in the workplace and at home can benefit from the rapidly growing availability of innovative applications for mobile devices.
- **Sensors are being embedded everywhere.** Low cost sensors embedded everywhere are enabling real-time data on temperature, airflow, system usage, etc., for every system and subsystem in the value chain.
- **Moving beyond spreadsheets.** Organizations are adopting purpose-built applications and databases to better respond to sustainability-related decision challenges requiring actionable data that is timely, granular, analyzable, and distributed to the edge.

Principles

- **Support decision making.** Sustainability is a decision-making challenge. Choosing to create sustainability is only the beginning—thereafter, staff at all levels in the organization will be faced with daily decision-making challenges. Better information will enable making decisions that better support sustainability.
- **Make data visible.** External stakeholders, executives, and front-line employees can make better decisions when they can see the sustainability-related performance in their areas of concern and when they get feedback on the results of their actions.
- **Leverage analytics.** Low cost sensors embedded everywhere across an organization's value chain provide huge streams of data to go along with the data being produced by business systems. This data can be hugely valuable, but only if analytic tools are used to help people make sense of it.
- **Exploit leverage points.** Because the market, business model, strategy, and location of each organization are different, the most valuable places to invest in sustainability will be different for each organization. IT can help to identify and then exploit those high leverage points.
- **Get actionable (timely, granular, analyzable) data to the edge.** Empower local leaders and individual contributors with the information they need to drive sustainability in their area. Ensure they can focus on analyzing and acting on data as opposed to collecting and reporting it.

Additional Resources

- **Business model innovation and sustainability.** A series of reports jointly authored by the MIT Sloan Management Review and the Boston Consulting Group present research on hundreds of companies and show how "companies that see sustainability as both an opportunity and necessity, and change their business models in response, are finding success."[22]

- **Software suppliers.** Sustainability software companies often have white papers and product brochures available on their websites that describe their offerings and how their customers are using them.

- **Research and advisory firms.** IT research and advisory firms such as Gartner and Forrester increasingly are providing good coverage of IT for sustainability offerings. In addition, sustainability-focused research firms such as Verdantix and Groom Energy are increasingly addressing IT issues. These firms make their money by charging for access to their materials, but they typically have a sampling of materials available for free download.

CHAPTER 5

Nurture a Culture of Sustainability

Introduction

The challenge of sustainability is such that it cannot be achieved by any one project or even by a set of projects. Each individual in an organization makes tens of decisions each day that either move toward sustainability or move away from it. Progress of the organization is paced by these decisions, and the extent to which an organization is a force for sustainability is determined by the extent to which each of its members is engaged with sustainability, by the extent to which the organization has a culture of sustainability. The more that sustainability becomes the job of everyone in IT, the more IT will contribute to the sustainability of the company or agency and the more it will be a net contributor to global sustainability.

"Embedded sustainability" is a term coined by Chris Lazlo and Nadya Zhexembayeva in their book with that title. While their book addresses a variety of business strategy issues, their discussion term is particularly helpful here for its description of a culture of sustainability—it is a culture in which employees choose to "embed sustainability into the DNA of what they do, incorporating environmental, health and social value into core business activities ...".[1] Sustainability in such a culture is not a "bolt-on" that is pursued in addition to their normal activities, or in spite of them, but rather is integral to how they provide value to their company or agency. Lazlo and Zhexembayeva's experience working with companies leads them to the lesson learned that embedding sustainability is a messy process. "Unlike the streamlined and often linear steps taken for bolt-on sustainability efforts, the task of embedding social and environmental value into the DNA of a business is iterative, repetitive, and chaotic. It demands new thinking and unorthodox solutions that can spring from unlikely sources and in improbable ways."

Ends

The third strategic end in our framework is to nurture a culture of sustainability within the IT organization. The verb nurture could be replaced by "create" or "build," but I like nurture because it captures the thought that a true culture of sustainability can't be dictated or forced. This intent, though subtle, is essential because the dimensions of the sustainability challenge exceed what can be addressed by any finite set of projects and initiatives. With respect to breadth or scope of activity, only if each member of the IT staff is engaged with the thought process of determining how IT operations can be more sustainable or how IT can help its partners to be more sustainable will it be possible to identify all the opportunities. While the organization will need to manage a portfolio of projects and must limit the number of projects funded and staffed at any one time, having every staff member engaged in identifying opportunities will enhance the list of candidates for funding and enhance the specification and implementation of funded and staffed projects. In addition, as the staff becomes engaged with sustainability, they will identify many opportunities that they can act on without proposing and getting approval for a project. For example, data center staff can make small adjustments to airflow patterns that reduce the energy needed for cooling, business analysts can asks additional questions when interviewing customers that lead to capturing sustainability requirements, those selecting suppliers can include sustainability factors, and end user services staff can configure desktop computers to better conserve energy.

To put a finer point on the end of nurturing a culture of sustainability, let's now look at several specific aspects that will characterize success in doing so.

Self-sustaining

The time-horizon of sustainability exceeds the scope of even the most long-ranging project portfolio. Sustainability is a journey that our organizations and humanity itself will be undertaking for many generations and only by creating a self-sustaining culture of sustainability can an organization ensure that the portfolio of sustainability projects will constantly be refreshed and that sustainability criteria are continually applied across the full spectrum of project and operations activities. The long-term nature of the challenge also means that sustainability-related learning will need to be an ongoing task for both individuals and the organization itself. An initial set of training activities can serve to jump-start the culture, but as with other projects, learning opportunities will need to be continually identified and leveraged long past the timeline of any existing training plans.

IT Staff as Exemplars

To the extent that the culture of the IT organization becomes an exemplar of sustainability, it will be an asset in making IT a partner for sustainability because it can serve as a catalyst for evolving the culture of the company as a whole, the culture of the IT industry, and the culture of the communities in which IT staff live. Because IT is embedded in just about all aspects of a modern business, IT staff have opportunities to influence just about everyone in the company by their actions and by what they communicate. The IT industry is famously fluid and thus open to influence by its members. And the cultures of our communities are not static, nor are they driven solely by outside influence. Rather, they are shaped on a daily basis by the attitudes and activities of their members and IT staff and their families can be as influential as they choose to be.

Synergy with Other Cultural Goals

Three additional benefits of developing a culture of sustainability within the IT organization deserve special mention and are closely related to each other. The first is that an increasing number of people are consciously seeking to work for an organization that has such a culture and so creating one is increasingly becoming an important means of recruiting and maintaining talent. A second benefit that is closely related to the first is that for this population a culture of sustainability in the workplace will lead to a greater level of employee engagement overall. Being able to connect their workplace with their desire to create sustainability can lead to their being more willing to engage more of their full selves with the mission of the organization. For many, sustainability is a cause that motivates the full application of one's creative energies. It justifies a level of commitment beyond that of an economic requirement to have a job. A third related benefit is that a culture of sustainability will provide pull for enhancing a culture of innovation. The sustainability challenge is in large part an innovation challenge, so as the organization seeks to create sustainability at every level and at every scale, it will create pull for innovation at every level and every scale. It will get people thinking about innovation and about removing barriers to innovation. A great large-scale example of this can be seen at GE. According to the program's vice president, Mark Vachon, GE's ecoimagination program has led not only to a big portfolio of successful products and services but also to unprecedented levels of innovation and engagement among engineering and technologists across the full scope of a massive company.[2]

Challenges

Perhaps, especially with culture-related goals, it is important to consider likely challenges before embarking on an initiative. The challenges to achieving a culture of sustainability in your organization may include these inter-related issues:

- **Employee skepticism about leadership commitment.** Employees who have been around awhile may have reason to believe that sustainability is simply the "program of the month" that will go away eventually and so is better ignored or complied with to the minimal extent possible.
- **Skepticism about the idea of sustainability.** Some employees are likely to believe that global warming, running out of resources, and so on are simply left-wing hoaxes or forms of hysteria. Some may think that whatever the reality of sustainability issues, it is not something that the company use time and money to address.
- **Perceived futility.** A related challenge is the thinking that while the challenges may be real, our ability to do anything about them is limited—"it won't make a difference anyway so why bother."

TEN Cycle

Pursuing a positive cycle of transparency, engagement, and networking (TEN) in support of nurturing a culture of sustainability can involve the following:

Transparency

- **Transparency about both successes *and* failures** of the IT sustainability program is essential to building a vital culture. The more visibility that employees have into what is working and what is not, the more they can engage in efforts to make things work better.
- **Providing access to data** that makes visible the sustainability-related impact of day-to-day decision making by IT staff is a key enabler of cultural change. Like Prius drivers, IT staff who get rapid feedback on how their actions increase or decrease energy use are naturally motivated to adjust their actions so as to reduce energy use.

Engagement

- **Engage all levels.** The more that employees at all levels can be engaged in creating the new culture, the stronger that creation will be. What you don't want is for the culture to be something that is simply "fanned out" and experienced by most employees as yet another "program of the month."
- **Enable employees to make the program their own.** Truly engaging employees means being open to their making the program their own, bringing their own notions about goals and ways and means to the mix.

Networking

- **Build relationships with sustainability programs in other functions** or with company-wide programs that address employee engagement. For example, site management teams may host Earth Day and would welcome IT participation.
- **Build relationships with community organizations.** There are likely to be employees who are members of sustainability-related

organizations in the community or who participate in community events. These employees can be a means of integrating the IT sustainability community into the network of these external groups.

Ways and Means

The ways and means of nurturing a culture of sustainability are similar to those for any positive cultural change initiative. In fact, as we explore more fully below, in most organizations opportunities exist to extend existing change programs so that they support sustainability goals. There are also opportunities to embed sustainability concerns into the standard processes and routine meetings of IT organizations, and, as with any cultural goal, success will depend in large part on leadership making the goals and communicating them as part of their formal and informal messaging.

Organize and Align

Because nurturing a culture of sustainability will be a long-term journey, it is important to establish enough organization to persevere in the iterative and repetitive tasks that will be required. This means that the top-level responsibility for working toward this end should be assigned to someone, most likely as just a part of their job, and regular reporting on progress and plans should be set up.

It will also be critically important to establish alignment vertically and horizontally. With respect to the vertical though there may not be any company- or agency-level initiatives specifically focused on the sustainability culture; there are likely to be other corporate culture initiatives on diversity, employee engagement, quality, community service, innovation, or similar themes that are relevant. If so, it will be absolutely essential that IT sustainability programs do not conflict with any of these efforts, but instead contribute to their success while also leveraging them for the purposes of the sustainability culture.

Examples of synergies with other cultural initiatives include:

- **Lean or six-sigma programs** are likely to emphasize engaging employees in efforts to eliminate waste. This can be leveraged by adding a focus on energy and water waste and by recognizing the sustainability-related gains that come out of the lean or six sigma projects.

- **Community engagement programs** encourage employees' involvement with local community projects and can be a source of personal sustainability practices (discussed later in this chapter) for employees. The same would be true for a program that encourages employees to adopt healthier lifestyles.
- **Innovation programs** can support efforts to innovate more environmentally efficient processes within IT and solutions for IT customers that help them with their sustainability challenges.

Horizontal alignment is also valuable with peer functions to IT that have significant roles in shaping the organizational culture. Examples of potential functional partners include:

- **Communications**—can help to craft and deliver messages to employees and may have guidelines that must be followed
- **HR**—may be able to add sustainability topics into new-hire orientations or build sustainability criteria into performance reviews
- **Training**—may be able to develop or purchase sustainability focused courses or even a full curriculum
- **Facilities**—may have programs for engaging employees at sites in recycling, energy and water use reduction, or sustainable commuting

Leadership Messaging

Leadership messaging is perhaps the largest lever for driving a culture toward (or away from) sustainability. This messaging includes formally presented messages and the messages sent informally as well as intentionally and unintentionally sent messages. To a large extent, the assessments that employees make about the extent to which sustainability is important to their organization will be determined by their readings of management messages. Employees have almost an automatic system for monitoring the content and frequency of where management really is on any issue and adjust their own thoughts and behaviors accordingly.

A key enabler, therefore, for creating a culture of sustainability is to ensure that IT leaders at all levels have the knowledge they need to be effective advocates for the IT sustainability program. They need to know how the IT program supports the larger goals of the company or agency, the achievements of the program so far, and about plans for the future. And they need to be aware of how much sustainability matters to some of their employees and to many in the communities in which they live and work.

To really be effective in moving the culture, leaders will also need to develop an understanding of what sustainability means to them personally. The more that a leader has reflected on why sustainability matters to him or her and its implications for thoughts and actions, the more that leader will be able to effect real change toward the end of nurturing a culture of sustainability. Leaders who make sustainability their own will naturally send messages that encourage their employees to do so as well. There is nothing wrong with preparing remarks and presentations for leaders to deliver and there is real value in doing so, but enabling them to put things in their own words will be even more valuable.

Means of enabling leaders to be drivers of the culture range from basic briefings or reports to them that provide them with information about the program, to providing materials and talking points that they can use in meetings with their teams, to facilitating workshops or other events in which they have the opportunity to deepen their understanding and reflect on how to make sustainability part of their personal visions. These sessions need not be long and can be included as part of the agenda in regular leadership team meetings. There are likely to be staff within your organization, and many external resources as well, who could facilitate such sessions. Sending out books such as this one can also be a means of supporting IT leaders in their sustainability journeys.

And finally, encourage leaders to ask questions about sustainability and to notice sustainability progress or its absence. They can do this at work by asking questions in project or operations reviews and when they are managing by walking around, to use the old phrase. And encourage them not to limit their questions and observations to the workplace but rather to practice asking questions about sustainability and notice sustainability across the range of their experiences. In particular, it is good to encourage them to notice the rapidly growing use of IT for sustainability in just about every domain, from personal and household activities to heavy industry and large cities (a number of these uses are described elsewhere in this book, but the variety and number in use are growing rapidly). Other focus areas to suggest include news about IT causing environmental harm through e-waste or energy use, sustainability affecting the competitiveness of companies or cities, and the sustainability-related material taught being taught to their children.

Identify and Connect Champions

In addition to the leaders designated as such on organization charts, there are many potential informal sustainability leaders throughout the larger organization. Identifying, connecting, and empowering already motivated individuals is a proven way to accelerate any cultural change and is particularly effective in the realm of sustainability. It is hard to imagine an IT organization today that doesn't already have members who are experimenting with solar energy, improving their recycling rate, or participating in the cleanup of a natural site near where they live. And many of these folks will already be thinking about how to reduce the energy use of IT equipment they work with and wondering about how the company can minimize its e-waste stream.

One way of identifying these individuals is simply to pay attention and make note when they self-identify themselves. Those who ask a question in a department meeting presentation of sustainability, those who make a suggestion, and even those who make a complaint about a lack of sustainability in some domain are already attempting to make the culture more sustainable. Another way of identifying the people you are looking for is a series of targeted surveys. The first survey is sent to a list of known sustainability champions and simply asks them for the names of folks that they interact with related to sustainability. This same survey is then sent to the new names identified by the initial respondents and the process is repeated as long as it is productive. In addition to building up a list of those interested, the surveys can be used to perform a social network analysis to identify who are the most influential "brokers" of this sustainability network by virtue of their being identified as a go to person by many others.

As folks are identified, it is important to connect them with the program and with each other. Means of connecting with them with the program can be as simple as adding them to a mailing list and sending out some information from time to time. Potential means of further strengthening the relationship include setting up recognition programs that provide a designation such as "Sustainability Citizen" for those who sign up to uphold a set of values or practices. If the company has some of the social platform systems discussed earlier in Chapter 4, these platforms can provide another great means of maintaining a connection between the sustainability program and its advocates and will also enable the individuals to connect with each other.

Going to the next level, formally supported communities of practice or communities of interest are an especially strong means of enabling connection with and between the sustainability advocates. The focus of these communities and their events can range from a broad look at global sustainability to very focused IT issues such as energy use in data centers. Whatever the focus, however, a great means of building a true sense of community is to encourage members to share their personal sustainability practices (PSPs). For those who are engaged with sustainability, learning from others who share their passions is a strong motivation to connect with them and to reach out to others. Learning that the database analyst down the hall is becoming an expert at composting or that a project manager is experimenting with solar panels will be very energizing for those with similar interests and translates into a strong motivation to connect more strongly with the workplace.

In addition to identifying and connecting self-selected sustainability advocates, it is important to empower them to make a difference in the workplace. In large part, this means responding to their suggestions and supporting them in trying out their ideas. Of course, not all ideas will be implementable, but in each case as they raise an idea it is important to respond to it. IT people understand that there are many constraints in their environment and can accept an answer like "Thanks for your thinking about how to reduce energy use on our desktops, but we are unable to implement that particular software because it conflicts with our anti-virus tools. However, we are looking at other similar tools and we will include you in that process and look forward to your contributions." The main thing is to avoid the engagement destroying act of not responding at all once someone has taken the initiative to make a suggestion. Suggestions may come in that are more related to another function such as facilities or

HR than IT and much good can come from helping the submitter to connect with the other function to explore their idea.

Promote PSPs

A goal of any cultural change initiative is for employees to embrace the desired change for themselves—to "make it their own." A great thing about moving toward a culture of sustainability is this is truly possible and many employees will choose to do so as it relates not only to their work lives but also to their homes and communities. One way to support this is to encourage employees to develop their own PSP. As the practices are personal, the choice of the practice should be wide open and the connection to sustainability should be as defined by the person. Examples might range from a very IT-specific work practice such as a technician being careful of how desktop energy management settings are configured, to turning off lights in unused conference rooms, to composting at home. Practices do not need to be limited to those that address environmental concerns and might include volunteering with a community social service organization or adopting new habits that will benefit a family's health.

Walmart, in partnership with the Clinton Global Initiative, provides a royalty-free license to a complete program they have implemented called My Sustainability Plan (MSP) that can "help your organization make personal sustainability an active part of daily life for your employees and stakeholders."[3] The license includes branding and a program framework: "Personal sustainability means something different to everyone, and MSP takes that into account with a program framework that offers something for everyone. MSP consists of 12 focus areas that span three categories—My Health, My Planet and My Life—that were developed with insights from people around the world." It also includes a curriculum: "MSP is all about setting goals to turn today's new habits into tomorrow's new lifestyles. But while making a commitment to change is a great first step, sticking with it is the hard part. The MSP curriculum provides helpful resources to help you stick with your goals. The curriculum is available in English as well as several other languages." Employees are able create and track their MSP goals on an online site and also see what others are doing. Additional means of encouraging PSPs include:

- Have individuals share their PSP in the community of practice or staff meetings.
- Publish short articles about individuals and their PSPs on the intranet.
- Encourage leaders to adopt PSPs and then to tell the story including the challenges they encountered and how adopting a PSP has benefited them personally.
- Encourage employees to share their PSPs on internal social media.

Embed Sustainability into IT Processes and Agendas

Most IT organizations have standard processes or methodologies that define the service life cycle and establish the requirements or "gates" to pass through successive phases such as project funding approval, requirements assessment, supplier selection, preliminary design, transition to production, and so on. In many cases, checklists are provided that specify criteria that must be addressed, subject matter experts who must review, and stakeholders who must approve.

These processes shape the culture in a real way because they define artifacts that must be created, conversations that must be held, and issues that must be thought through. Inserting sustainability concerns into them is thus a great way to ensure that sustainability thinking becomes part of the daily rhythm of the workgroups in the organization. They also provide management with opportunities re-enforce the messages about their commitment to sustainability. For example, not granting an approval to proceed to development because sustainability criteria were not properly addressed in the requirements sends a strong message—"we're about sustainability"—that will be sent rapidly through the organization.

Examples of potential insertions of sustainability criteria into the methodology include:

- **Product selection.** Product criteria such as the EPEAT and Energy Star certifications discussed in Chapter 3 and the sustainability performance of the supplier itself can be considered. Do they have a sustainability strategy? Do they report carbon emissions?
- **Application design.** Energy-use criteria can be part of evaluating an application design. Is the code efficient? Will the application run in our virtualized environment?

- **Infrastructure design.** Energy-use criteria also apply to infrastructure design. Is the environment sized appropriately? Is the level of redundancy truly required? Were cloud-based alternatives considered?

The regular meetings of IT departments often have standard agendas to which placeholders for sustainability topics can be added. Examples of inserting sustainability topics into standard meeting agendas include:

- Information on sustainability progress in meetings held to discuss company or agency financials, goal achievement, market, etc.
- Sustainability metrics as part of standing operations reviews
- Presentations by employees on their PSPs
- In partner review meetings with key IT supplier, add discussions of the suppliers' sustainability program and of how their products or services will contribute to your program
- Sustainability contributions can be added to the criteria considered in promotion review boards.

Project reviews are particularly great leverage points for changing the culture—teams soon learn to be ready for the questions that will be asked in them and so regularly asking sustainability-related questions will drive sustainability thinking into the organization. Questions that are appropriate at various phases in the project life cycle include:

- How did you factor in sustainability performance when you picked your supplier?
- Is the hardware you selected EPEAT certified? How does its energy use compare with the other products you considered?
- Are you planning to implement this application on virtual servers? If not, why not?
- What will happen to these devices at their end-of-life?
- Can we turn off any applications when we turn this one on?

In organizations that have well-documented methodologies, questions like these can be embedded into formal checklists.

Leverage Lean, Six Sigma, and Diversity Programs

Programs such as lean, six sigma, or diversity, when they exist in an organization, are strong drivers of organizational culture and can be effective levers for nurturing a culture of sustainability. For example, most lean programs emphasize the importance of eliminating waste and teach employees to identify the "seven deadly wastes" such as overproduction, transportation, defects, and so on. A straightforward addition to this training is to add a focus on leaning to see the environmental aspects of these wastes. Overproduction, for example, means that more raw materials and energy are consumed in making the unnecessary products, extra products may spoil or become obsolete requiring disposal, and extra hazardous materials used result in extra emissions, waste disposal, worker exposure, etc.

A natural extension of six sigma programs that, typically, emphasize the continuous pursuit of perfection is to show employees how this can easily be extended to goals such as eliminating any harmful disposal of e-waste. Another natural extension is to show how using data to prioritize improvement efforts can be applied to, for example, identifying the most valuable place to focus energy-use reduction efforts. Diversity programs also typically have content that can be easily extended—learning about the PSPs of others can be added to the curriculum on valuing the diversity of other employees, for example.

Provide Feedback Data

In Chapter 4, we discussed how IT can be used to provide feedback to individual employees and teams on the sustainability impact of their actions and it is as important to do this for IT employees as it is anywhere else in the organization. Just as a scale can help us change our eating habits or the dashboard on a Prius can help lead to a change in driving habits, so too can providing timely data that is at the right level of granularity support changes in behavior in the IT workplace. A data center manager who can see the daily impact of his or her decisions on energy use will naturally try to find ways to optimize that use, and a storage engineer who can see how his or her choices contribute to the data center energy goals will be far more likely to consider energy use when choosing products or configuring systems.

Promote Continuous Learning

Promoting continuous learning related to sustainability is a key way of ensuring that the culture continues to progress and counter plateaus. While it is great if everyone gets the message that they need to use virtual servers and turn the lights off at night, if employees become complacent and think that they've "got it" then progress will be limited and will likely falter at some point. On the other hand, if employees begin to see that there is always more to learn, they will begin to experience sustainability as a life-long journey, and when this occurs for more and more employees, the culture will be propelled irreversibly toward sustainability.

The good news associated with the sometimes overwhelming challenges of sustainability is that there is always something new to learn about the challenges and about how to address them. A steady flow of new information is emerging daily on topics ranging from the science, to politics and policy, to technology, to business models and practices, to psychology and personal practices. There is truly something for everybody who is at all interested in the topic.

And of course these days there is also a tremendous range of media options to support learning. These range from face-to-face classroom training to virtual real-time or asynchronous classes, to conferences, to webinars, to on-demand podcasts, to twitter hashtags, to ebooks and even printed books. All of these are relevant for sustainability-related learning and are being used as channels by an ever-increasing number of content providers. More and more universities offer both degrees and short programs; management and sustainability specialist consulting companies offer research materials and training; IT suppliers offer webinars on how companies have used their products; and social media provides a steady stream of insights, links, and discussions.

In addition to the many options for content and delivery, options also exist with respect to how an organization promotes and supports their use by employees. The spectrum of these options can best be understood as ranging from push to pull. The strongest form of push options include mandatory training or training delivered as part of all-employees meetings. Pull options include, most obviously, letting folks find things on the Internet for themselves, but can also include negotiating with training suppliers for online or live training for which employees can enroll, providing and publicizing events with speakers or workshops, providing materials in internal libraries or on the intranet, and providing edited sets of links to the most relevant of the many resources available externally. Another way to support pull is by recognizing those who obtain degrees, certificates, or other credentials.

Promote Innovation

Promoting innovation is an important way to nurture a culture of sustainability. To innovate is to introduce something new into the workplace, the supply chain, the market, or the community, and the value of innovation is obvious not just for sustainability but also for business success generally. However, in spite of its value, many organizations do not promote innovation in a significant way. Either they have no program to do so at all, or they have a program "on paper" that does not have any real energy behind it. The primary reason for this common state of affairs, I believe, is that managers are needlessly discouraged from focusing on innovation because innovation is equated with achieving "game changers" such as creating the next iPhone. While some organizations do in fact have such a goal, for many this seems to be outside the realm of possibility and so innovation is given an occasional mention, but is otherwise neglected. Fight or flight is an understandable response by either managers or their employees to the expectation of finding a multimillion dollar idea.

The antidote to this discouragement is a better understanding of innovation. Introducing something new to a workplace or a product line does not mean that the something needs to be big, nor does it mean that it needs to be completely new under the sun. Taking an idea that you get at an open house at your child's school and applying it in the office is innovation because it results in a new condition in the workplace. Making a small improvement to a production process is innovation because it contributes overtime to large improvements, as demonstrated by the Toyota Production System and its imitations.

In fact, as Dr. Robert Maurer, a UCLA psychologist teaches, the best way to create a culture of innovation is through encouraging small changes. Rather than asking for the next big thing, he suggests asking employees "what's the smallest possible improvement we could make?"[4] This approach gets the ball rolling because it reduces the level of fear for both employees and managers. It also introduces a way of thinking that employees can use in every aspect of their work and personal lives. Positive responses to consequential challenges such as losing weight to lower one's blood pressure or the imperative to minimize global warming are often inhibited by fear. Finding a way to start that doesn't trigger feelings of fear can be extremely powerful.

To keep the ball rolling, it is essential to pay attention to the suggestions that people make, to the questions they ask, and to the improvements they make. A large reward is not required to encourage suggestions, but not responding to those that are made will quickly stop the process of making them. The response to an idea may have to be that it can't be implemented for some policy or practical reason, but even that response if combined with an explanation and sincere thank you will encourage the next one. The program office must itself notice and respond to initiatives taken by employees and should also encourage IT managers across the organization to do so as well.

Rewards and Recognition

Key to any cultural change initiative is to recognize when people take action in the direction of the desired change. This can include formal rewards and recognition for major accomplishments, but it should also include recognizing small changes when they occur. For example, verbal recognition in the moment of the fact that a participant in a design review asked about energy use will lead to more such questions in future reviews. Or, noting that a data center manager took the initiative to raise the temperature in a center by a degree or two will encourage others to do the same.

Summary

Trends

- **Caring is increasing.** More employees and potential employees care about sustainability. Employees are placing more value on the opportunity to be engaged with sustainability programs in their workplace.

- **Networks based on passions and interests.** People are seeking out others for mutual support on common interests and passions more actively than ever before.5
- **Increasing resources.** Resources (both content and channels) for continuous learning about sustainability are increasing rapidly.

Principles

- **Identify and connect potential champions.** Just about all IT organizations today have employees who are already passionate about sustainability. Connecting them with the program and with each other will provide instant and sustained energy.
- **Leverage leadership.** There is no substitute for the role of leadership messaging and behaviors in driving culture change of any type.
- **Notice and recognize contributions.** Paying attention to those who make suggestions or even make actual improvements is the best way to ensure that more of the same will follow.
- **Support small changes.** Making large changes in our organizations or in our personal lives often requires starting with a small change, just as the direction of a large ship must be changed by moving the trim tab, which makes it possible to turn the rudder and then the ship.
- **Connect sustainability with innovation.** Creating sustainability requires and drives innovation. It means creating something new in the enterprise and many employees will want to connect their own creativity with this process.
- **Connect sustainability with existing continuous improvement programs.** Six sigma, lean, or employee engagement programs that already exist are already providing sustainability-related benefits and can themselves be strengthened in return by the IT sustainability program.

Additional Resources

- *Our Iceberg Is Melting.* A recent book by one of the most prominent authorities on cultural change, John Kotter, is very relevant to sustainability culture. Kotter's firm also provides a variety of training resources that go along with the book.[6]

- **The Natural Step.** The Natural Step is a well-established sustainability not-for-profit organization providing low-cost overview training on sustainability that can provide a means for educating employees on the basic ideas of sustainability and also offers more advanced materials.[7]

CHAPTER 6

Maintain Forward Progress

Oscillating Versus Creating

Sustainability is by definition a challenge for the long term. After we have launched an IT sustainability program and it is trimming IT's footprint, is engaging with other functions to address their footprints, and perhaps is even exploring how IT might contribute to product and service offerings that address the sustainability goals of customers, we will have created significant momentum. The question that then needs to be addressed is how do we maintain this momentum for the long term? The situation at this point is somewhat like that of a person who realized they wanted to loose weight, began a diet, and is in fact losing some weight. At this point, they need to ask how will they ensure they continue to do so until they reach their goal, and then most challenging of all, how will they stay at their desired weight for the long term and avoid the fate of so many, of gaining back most of their original weight and finding themselves needing to select a new diet and to begin again?

The analogy to permanent weight loss is not perfect—getting to the 2050 vision will take considerably more changes over a significantly longer period of time—but it does provide a means to illustrate the underlying structural issues that will determine whether progress is sustained over the long term, or whether our weight, actual or metaphorical, returns. It is structure, not will power or luck, that is determinate and we all experience this ourselves in some aspect of life. Most of us know someone who has experienced this in the area of weight loss. They were as determined as could be to reach and maintain their weight goal and made a great start, but after loosing many pounds and getting close to their goal, they seem to get pulled back toward their previous weight as surely as if they were on a swing that had reached the top of its arc and is being pulled back the other way. Similarly, those who have worked in large companies or governmental organizations are likely to have experienced the "change program of the month" where quality or diversity or efficiency programs have been rolled out with great fanfare and early progress only to be ultimately rejected and largely forgotten by the organization.

Those familiar with the work of Robert Fritz will have realized by now that I am making reference here to the principle that he has explicated in several books and that he teaches along with his wife Rosalind in workshops and consulting engagements. The principle is that structure determines behavior, and Fritz illustrates it by reminding us that the path that water on a hill takes as it flows to meet the river in the valley and out to the sea is determined not by the will of the water molecules, but by the structure of the hillside. This structure determines where small streams will develop and where they will meet and form brooks, and so on—water, as Fritz puts in the title of one of his books, follows the *path of least resistance*. This is to state the obvious for water on a hill, but Fritz's not-so-obvious insight here is that determinative structures also exist in our lives, and no matter how much positive thinking or will power we might employ, when push comes to shove, we will end up following the path of least resistance as determined by these structures.

There is one big difference between water molecules and us, however—we can choose to shape the structures that will drive our behavior. We can create structures for ourselves that lead to continued advancement toward our chosen goals and that replace the default structures typically in place, which produce oscillating patterns that make us feel we are on a swing set. We can create a structure for ourselves in which we are pulled toward our desired ends, in which the "structural tension," as Fritz puts it, between our current state and that of our desired state is such that the path of least resistance will be to advance rather than to oscillate. And we can disassemble the default structure in which the structural tension pulling us back toward our starting point grows stronger as we get closer to our goal, thus causing us to oscillate.

Maintain Personal Momentum

Below we will look at the application of Fritz's thought to our organizations, but first we need to look at the importance of his model of structural tension for each of us in our roles as individual change agents. Whether we are in an IT organization trying to get it to do more work on its own footprint, or whether we are in another function attempting to bring IT to bear on our efforts to move our organization toward sustainability, it will be vital to consider the structural dynamics of our own personal situations. To be effective in keeping our organization advancing, we need to keep advancing ourselves.

In order to do this, we need to establish structures for ourselves that lead to advancement rather than to oscillation. To some extent, the goal structures that you've helped create for the organization will provide pull to keep you moving in the direction of the organization's goals, and it will help you to be much more resilient in the face of the inevitable setbacks, delays, mistakes, failures, complaints, and so on that are part of organizational life to maintain structural tension for yourself at the scale of your own life and career. And to the extent that you and others in the organization do this for themselves, it will make the organization as a whole more resilient and effective.

The key to creating and maintaining structural tension for yourself is to develop clear pictures of what you want to create in your life and hold these in tension with your current reality. It is precisely this tension, between what you want to create and what exists today, that will pull you toward achieving what you want to achieve. One essential part of the process is to ensure that you have clarity about what you want to create and that you make conscious decisions about the relationships between competing goals. Advancement toward a goal will be compromised just as it seems to be in reach if getting close to the goal is pulling you away from another goal. Examples of such structures that Fritz uses include the tension between maintaining stability in your life versus introducing change, or the common tension between short-term and long-term goals. When a clear hierarchical relationship (i.e., clarity about what is more important) between such competing goals is not established, the result will be oscillation between the goals rather than advancement. For the dieter, this would mean getting close to a weight goal only to fall back to the comfort of previous lifestyle habits and the weight that comes with them. For a change agent, it might mean making a bit of a dent only to fall back into the security of not rocking the boat. On the other hand, having clarity about your goals and how they relate will enable you to be resilient in the face of the inevitable setbacks, delays, complaints, failures, and so on that are part of the change process.

Continuous Learning

Another key to maintaining your progress over the long haul will be continuous learning. Of particular importance here will be learning that supports the maintenance of structural tension as described above. One of the benefits that I hope you are getting from reading this book is a growing awareness of the ever-growing set of opportunities to make IT operations more sustainable and the even more rapidly growing number of opportunities to leverage IT to make other business processes more sustainable. I'm hopeful that as you go through your day you are noticing applications of technology being made in other organizations and wondering if your organization could do something similar. When the next big thing is announced by the IT industry (which often seems to be a weekly occurrence), I'm hoping that you will be giving a bit of thought to how it might be applied to create sustainability.

Such observation and reflection is a great form of continuous learning and will happen naturally from now on, almost in spite of yourself, as you encounter the numerous sources of information to which you are already exposed. For those of you who want to further accelerate your learning and strengthen your structural tension, I want to share here some of the online resources that are updated regularly and that provide daily fodder for my ongoing learning.

- **The Green IT Review** (http://www.thegreenitreview.com/): Pete Foster authors this blog, which provides solid information on one or two important IT-related developments on a daily basis.
- **The Guardian Low Carbon IT Hub** (http://www.guardian.co.uk/sustainable-business/hubs-low-carbon-ict): Backed by the UK's *Guardian* newspaper, this active site focuses on IT and business issues related to sustainability.
- **Greentech Pastures** (http://www.zdnet.com/blog/green/): Authored by Heather Clancy, this blog is a great source for new IT and other technology developments relevant to sustainability.

- **Leanblog.org** (www.leanblog.org): This blog does not have a sustainability focus but it is one of the best resources for tracking the ongoing discussion about lean and there are often useful thoughts on how to reduce waste or how to build a healthy culture.
- **Dot Earth** (Dotearth.blogs.nytimes.com): Written by long-time environmental writer Andrew Revkin of the *New York Times*, this is the best resource I know for keeping current with global discourse on environmental sustainability. News items are discussed along with a balanced view of the discussion from various camps on such issues as the reality of global warming.
- **Environmentalleader.com** (www.environmentalleader.com): A good daily flow of news about the environment and related innovations with a focus on business and corporations.
- **Greenbiz** (greenbiz.com): This is a good "one-stop shopping" site for keeping abreast of environmental sustainability. A good-sized staff provides a good mix of new stories and columns by their own writers as well as links from the web.
- **IT research firms** such as Forrester and Gartner also have an increasing focus on sustainability and if your firm has a subscription to their service it will be well worthwhile to make sure that you leverage their sustainability research.

Leveraging Maturity Models

Maturity models are a well-established means of maintaining structural tension and forward progress in organizational change initiatives. One of the best-known examples of this is the Capability Model Maturity Integration (CMMI) developed and supported by Carnegie Mellon. It has been used in many IT shops and software development organizations across the globe both in industry and in government and has led to substantial improvements in how software is developed and the quality of the resulting software. Similar models often derived from the CMMI have been developed for many industries and some are now emerging that should prove to be valuable for sustainability efforts. A paper[1] describing one of these models, the "Business Sustainability Maturity Model" developed at the University of Manchester, has a nice description of how it supports the process of keeping a vision vital:

"The maturity model suggested is based on the belief that business sustainability is a continuous process of evolution in which a company will be continuously seeking to achieve its vision of sustainable development in uninterrupted cycles of improvement, where at each new cycle the firm starts the process at a higher level of business sustainability performance."

There are also IT sustainability-specific models and a valuable example of this is the Data Center Maturity Model (DCMM) developed by Green-Grid. It "aims to give a holistic view of data center sustainability and help organizations benchmark performance, determine levels of maturity, and identify ongoing steps and innovations to achieve greater energy efficiency in the future. On the facility side, DCMM breaks the data centre down into four categories: power, cooling, management and 'other' ... Similarly, on the IT side, DCMM breaks the data centre down into compute, storage, network and 'other'. Scores range from 0 to 5, 0 being 'minimal/no progress', 2 being 'best practice', and 5 being 'visionary'.."[2]

A model that addresses not just data centers, but the full spectrum of sustainable information and communications technologies (SICT) is the SICT-Capability Maturity Framework (SICT-CMF). This framework[3] defines a five-level maturity curve for identifying and developing SICT capabilities:

- **Initial:** SICT is ad hoc; there's little understanding of the subject and few or no related policies. Accountabilities for SICT aren't defined, and SICT isn't considered in the systems life cycle.
- **Basic:** There's a limited SICT strategy with associated execution plans. It's largely reactive and lacks consistency. There's an increasing awareness of the subject, but accountability isn't clearly established. Some policies might exist but are adopted inconsistently.
- **Intermediate:** An SICT strategy exists with associated plans and priorities. The organization has developed capabilities and skills and encourages individuals to contribute to sustainability programs. The organization includes SICT across the full systems life cycle, and it tracks targets and metrics on an individual project basis.
- **Advanced:** Sustainability is a core component of the IT and business planning life cycles. IT and business jointly drive programs and

progress. The organization recognizes SICT as a significant contributor to its sustainability strategy. It aligns business and SICT metrics to achieve success across the enterprise. It also designs policies to enable the achievement of best practices.

- **Optimizing:** The organization employs SICT practices across the extended enterprise to include customers, suppliers, and partners. The industry recognizes the organization as a sustainability leader and uses its SICT practices to drive industry standards. The organization recognizes SICT as a key factor in driving sustainability as a competitive differentiator.

Refreshing Goals and the Business Case

In order to maintain the structural tension needed to ensure continued progress as your initial goals are met, new goals will be required. One way to set new goals is simply to extend the initial goals—when the target of reducing data center power by 1 megawatt is reached, for example, simply set a goal for another megawatt. A related way of setting new goals is to broaden the domain being addressed. For example, you could add a focus on the energy being used by network facilities to an initial focus on computer and data centers.

A more challenging way of setting new goals, however, is to target some of the *characteristics* of the next level up on the maturity model that you are using. For example, one the levels in the DCMM is characterized by the statement that "the organization recognizes SICT (sustainable information and communications technology) as a significant contributor to its sustainability strategy." This characteristic presents a challenge for goal setting in that it will take some work to find a way to describe it in a way that progress against it can be measured. It may be worth struggling with this challenge, however, because the setting of such goals will lead to moving up the maturity model and to adding more value to your organization and to society as a whole.

Along with refreshing the goals, another essential requirement for maintaining forward progress will be to update the business case and how it is communicated. One obvious but important way to do this will be to incorporate the results that you have achieved so far into the story as proof points of what is possible in the future. Another way of leveraging your work for communicating the business case is to translate your growing understanding of the sustainability programs in other functions to messages about what IT can contribute and about the value of doing so. In fact, all of your ongoing learning about sustainability can also be brought to bear on evolving your business case messaging. The more that you understand about global sustainability challenges, about how other organizations are responding to them, about how new technologies are being applied, and about how your organization is could be responding to the challenges, the more that you can craft a compelling business case. As your learning deepens, you will have an ever-growing source of material to motivate your organization, your team, and yourself along what can be a life-long journey. I hope that this book has made a contribution to this process and wish you the very best as you go forward.

Summary

Trends

- Society continues to "raise the bar" with respect to the sustainability performance it expects from organizations.
- Resources for continuous learning by sustainability practitioners are increasing steadily.

Principles

- Maintain structural tension to keep yourself and your organization moving forward—continue to refresh your goals and your case for action.
- Strive to focus more on creating sustainability than on solving problems or reducing unsustainability.

Additional Resources

- Information on maintaining structural tension, including both written and online interactive materials based on the work of Robert Fritz, is available at www.robertfritz.com.

Glossary and Primer

2 Billion: The world's population in 1927 was 2 billion.

7 Billion: The world's population 2011 was 7 billion.

9 Billion: The world's population is projected to be 9 billion by 2050. See also **Vision 2050**.

450 ppm: 450 parts per million (ppm) of CO_2 in the atmosphere is a target intended to keep mean global temperature by 2100 to no more than 2°C above pre-industrial levels.

Application, App: Apps or applications are pieces of software that can run on servers in a data center, on a pc, on a personal device, or in the cloud. The ever-increasing use of apps by individuals, firms, and agencies will lead to ever-increasing energy use and e-waste if steps such as those presented in this book are not taken.

Bottom of the Pyramid: The bottom of the pyramid is a term used to refer to the estimated 2.5 billion people who live on less than $2.50 per day. See also **Vision 2050**.

Carbon Dioxide, CO_2: Expressed as CO_2, this is the gas that all animals breath out, that fertilizes the growth of plants, and that puts the fizz in club soda. It is also created when fossil fuels are burned, and as societies across the globe have increased their use of fossil fuels over the last 100 years, the amount of CO_2 in the atmosphere has increased from x to y, because the rate at which it is going into the atmosphere has exceeded the rate at which it is taken out of the atmosphere by plants, by the ocean, or by escaping into space. This is an issue because it is a greenhouse gas. While other gases such as methane are more potent greenhouse gases, CO_2 is the focus of much concern because of the vast quantities being placed into the atmosphere each year. In 2010, the quantity of CO_2 added was the greatest ever recorded, in spite of 20 years or more of efforts to reduce CO_2 emissions.

Carbon Caps/Carbon Trading: In the 1970s, the EPA successfully reduced the acid rain caused by sulfur dioxide pollution by instituting caps on the amount that a power generator could emit, but then allowing them to trade credits for that amount with other generators who could perhaps reduce their emissions more readily. This created a market that found the best way to allocate improvement funds while still meeting the necessary reduction targets. A similar idea has been proposed to manage CO_2 emissions, though it is yet to be widely adopted, because of the impact on costs throughout the economy. Carbon trading would have significant IT implications because of the importance of accurate accounting and reporting of carbon use.

Carbon Disclosure Project (CDP): The CDP is a non-profit organization that represents investors with assets totaling more that $40 trillion. Its regular surveys of the world's largest companies to assess risks and opportunities related to climate change is one of the drivers of the need for IT support for sustainability performance reporting.

Carbon Footprint: The amount of carbon dioxide equivalent greenhouse gases produced by an organization or process constitutes its carbon footprint. A **Personal Carbon Footprint** refers to the greenhouse gases that result from the actions of an individual.

Carbon Accounting: Carbon accounting refers to keeping track of the carbon released into the atmosphere as a result of the operations of an enterprise.

Cloud Computing: Cloud computing provides on-demand network access to a shared pool of computing resources (e.g., networks, servers, storage, applications, and services) that can be rapidly provisioned or released. Private clouds are operated exclusively for one firm. Public clouds involve a third party providing the cloud service that different firms share.

Conflict Metals, Conflict Minerals: Conflict minerals are mined in areas of armed conflict or human rights abuses, most prominently in the Democratic Republic of the Congo. The metals concerned, tantalum, tungsten, tin, and gold, are commonly used in electronics.

CUE: CUE stands for carbon usage effectiveness and is a sustainability metric for data centers. It extends the idea of power usage effectiveness (PUE) by adding in a factor for the carbon effectiveness of the power used for the data center. CUE can be calculated by multiplying the PUE for a data center against a carbon emission factor (CEF). So, CUE = PUE × CEF.

Data Centers: Essentially factories where large amounts of electricity are converted into the compute cycles that underlie most modern business processes and much of our personal computing use when it involves using a search engine, posting a video, or downloading a song.

Data Center Information Management (DCIM) Systems: DCIM tools monitor, measure, manage, and/or control data center utilization and energy consumption of all IT-related equipment (such as servers, storage, and network switches) and facility infrastructure components (such as power distribution units (PDUs) and computer room air conditioners (CRACs)).[1]

Dynamic Power Optimization (DPO): DPO improves data center energy efficiency by working with load balancing or virtualization software to continuously match server capacity with demand. This "on-demand" approach saves a great deal of energy as compared with the "always on" practice typical in most data centers.

E-waste: E-waste, or electronic waste, refers to electronic components that are discarded at the end of their use by an organization or individual. These components often contain hazardous materials such as lead and cadmium and also valuable materials such as gold, silver, and rare earth elements that can make recycling e-waste profitable.

Embedded Carbon, Embedded Water: Embedded carbon or water refers to the amount of carbon released into the atmosphere or the water used to manufacture and ship a product or build a structure.

Energy Monitoring Systems: For homeowners, companies are selling energy-monitoring services that show real-time energy use and suggest ways to reduce it.

Enterprise Smart Grid: Enterprise Smart Grid, a term coined by Groom Energy, is the application of smart grid concepts to the demand side as opposed to the supply side of energy production and distribution by utilities. Enterprise Smart Grid involves the use of submeters, demand response, energy management software, and building management systems to drive reduction in energy use within a company or agency.

Greenhouse Gases (GHGs): In a greenhouse, more of the energy from the sun can enter through the glass roof than can exit. Greenhouse gases function similarly around the earth and without them the earth would be too cold to support human life. Many are concerned, however, that global warming may result as the concentration of these gases grows due to modern industrial processes and the burning of fossil fuels. The GHGs include carbon dioxide (CO_2), methane (CH_4), nitrous oxide (N_2O), hydrofluorocarbons (HFCs), perfluorocarbons (PFCs), and sulfur hexafluoride (SF_6).

GHG Protocol: The Greenhouse Gas Protocol is the most widely used international accounting tool to understand, quantify, and manage GHG emissions. It is maintained by a partnership between the World Resources Institute and the World Business Council for Sustainable Development and provides the accounting framework for nearly every GHG standard and program in the world.

Intelligent Building Systems (IBS): Intelligent (or smart) building systems refer to the convergence of IT technologies with traditional building automation systems. They promise significant reduction in building energy and water usage.

Intelligent Transport Systems (ITS): Intelligent transportation systems "can make traffic flow more smoothly by controlling traffic lights to match changing conditions, advising drivers about hazards or jams ahead, using ramp meters to smoothly insert autos into traffic, or charging tolls on the fly electronically, to name just a few. Taking all these steps would cut fuel use by 5% and prevent 308 million person-hours of delay per year, worth $6.5 billion."

IT Estate: The IT estate refers to the entire suite of information technology that supports a business.

Life Cycle Analysis/Life Cycle Accounting (LCA): LCA provides information on the environmental impact of a product across its life cycle beginning with the sourcing of materials, through its manufacture, its use by a customer, and then its end-of-life disposition. Customer demand for this information is a significant driver of IT for sustainability investment.

Ocean Acidification: As CO_2 levels in the atmosphere increase, more CO_2 is absorbed by the oceans leading to several chemical reactions that increase the acidity of the water. This is an issue because it affects the growth of many organisms, especially those that live in shells, which can be dissolved by acidic water.

Platform as a Service (PaaS): A segment of cloud services that provides a development platform for the design and test of custom applications.

Private Cloud: A service operated exclusively for one firm. This service can be provided either internally or externally by a third-party provider.

Public Cloud: Public cloud services are provided on a multi-tenant basis, meaning that different firms share the same infrastructure, platform, or instance of the software application.

PUE: Power usage effectiveness is a data center efficiency measure; it calculates the ratio of the total power consumed by a data center against the total power consumed by the IT equipment. See also **CUE**.

REACH: The acronym stands for Registration, Evaluation, and Authorization of Chemicals. REACH takes precedence over most pre-existing EU Chemical Regulations. The responsible party for REACH is the manufacturer (if based in the EU) or the importer. The threshold quantities apply per manufacturer or importer, not per product line.

RoHS: Restriction of Hazardous Substances (RoHS) Directive, adopted in February 2003 by the European Union, is intended to reduce the effect of hazardous waste created by electronic products on the environment. The directive took effect on July 1, 2006, and places clear restrictions on the use of six hazardous materials used in the manufacture of electronic and electrical components.

Scope 1 Emissions: GHG emissions that are the direct result of company operations such as the burning of fossil fuels or manufacturing processes that emit a GHG such as methane or carbon dioxide.

Scope 2 Emissions: Scope 2 emissions are created at power utilities as a result of providing the electrical power used by a company. The quantity of these emissions for a given amount of power use can vary based upon the means by which the electricity is generated (i.e., coal, vs. gas, vs. nuclear, vs. wind, etc.).

Scope 3 Emissions: Companies in the supply chain create Scope 3 emissions when they create products or services for the parent organization.

Separation: In data centers, this refers to the practice of preventing the cool air that is intended to be used to cool servers from mixing with the hot air that is ejected from servers by their fans. One best practice for achieving this is to create hot aisles and cool aisles.

Server: A server is a computer dedicated to running one or more services available on a company intranet or on the Internet. In a data center, multiple servers are typically mounted in racks, which are arranged in rows. Virtualization allows one physical server to host multiple "virtual servers."

Server Virtualization: The creation of multiple server instances on one physical server machine enables significant increases in hardware utilization and efficiency. See **Virtualization**.

Smart Grid: The smart grid combines IT with the electric grid to enable consumers and industrial customers to optimize power buys and to enable providers to integrate renewables and enhance overall system efficiencies. "Information technology has driven remarkable innovations in how electricity can be monitored, controlled, and delivered. These 'smart grid' technologies not only can make the grid more reliable and secure, they can also make it more efficient, reducing the amount of power generation required in the first place. … Information technology providers are quickly infiltrating the electricity business with products that greatly enhance the level of information supplied to customers, utilities, and even energy using devices."[2]

Software as a Service (SaaS): SaaS refers to cloud computing services that provide applications through a centralized network allowing access over the Internet or intranet.

Virtualization: "Virtualization means to create a virtual version of a device or resource, such as a server, storage device, network or even an operating system where the framework divides the resource into one or more execution environments. … Devices, applications and human users are able to interact with the virtual resource as if it were a real single logical resource."[3] Virtualization can be applied to storage, servers, networks, operating systems, and applications. By utilizing virtualization, the utilization of the underlying physical resources can be greatly increased, which reduces energy use, the number of physical devices that have to be manufactured, and the potential for e-waste.

Virtual Private Cloud (VPC): A cloud service that is only accessible via a private network connection and not through the open Internet.

Vision 2050: "A world in which nine billion people can live well, and within the planet's resources, by mid-century" is the vision statement developed by the World Business Council for Sustainable Development.[4]

Notes

Preface

1. Hewlett-Packard (2013).
2. Gallagher (2013).
3. Lovins (2011).

Chapter 1

1. Willard (2012).
2. Senge (2010).
3. Ehrenfeld (2008).
4. World Business Council for Sustainable Development (2010).
5. Granatstein (2008).

Chapter 2

1. Yarger (2010).
2. Prominent examples of this include Stanford University (http://sustainablestanford.stanford.edu/sustainable_it) and Intel (http://www.intel.com/content/www/us/en/it-management/intel-it-management-role-in-sustainability-practices.html).
3. Werbach (2009).

Chapter 3

1. Werbach (2009).
2. PUE is the preferred energy efficiency metric for data centers. PUE is a measure of the total energy of the data center divided by the IT energy consumption. When calculating PUE, IT energy consumption should, at a minimum, be measured at the output of the uninterruptible power supply (UPS) and ideally directly at the IT load (i.e., servers). For a dedicated data center, the total energy in the PUE equation will include all energy sources at the point of utility handoff to the data center owner or operator. For a data center in a mixed?use building, the total energy

will be all energy required to operate the data center, similar to a dedicated data center, and should include IT energy, cooling, lighting, and support infrastructure for the data center operations. The PUE metric was developed by The Green Grid (www.thegreengrid.org), a nonprofit consortium that develops and shares information on how to make IT more resource efficient.

3. Emerson Network Power (2012).
4. Different means of generating electricity vary greatly in terms of how much green house gas emissions they produce. Compare, for example, hydro-generated electricity with coal-generated electricity.
5. Wikipedia (n.d.).
6. Ghandi (2012).
7. ASHRAE (2011).
8. Cappuccio (2010).
9. Pfeiffer (2011).
10. Environmental Leader (2012a).

Chapter 4

1. http://www.ghgprotocol.org
2. www.groomenergy.com
3. U.S. Department of Energy (2010).
4. Bartlett (2011).
5. Aston (2012).
6. Carter (2011).
7. www.energystar.gov/PortolioManager
8. Personal conversation with Peter Graf, CSO of SAP, July 15, 2011.
9. See www.patagonia.com/us/footprint
10. See http://www.unilever.com/sustainable-living/
11. Environmental Leader (2012b).
12. ASU (2012).
13. ASU (2012).
14. Lovins (2011).
15. Harris (2012b).
16. Harris (2012a).
17. Environmental Leader (2012c).
18. Tweed (2012).
19. Forhez (2008).
20. Siegel (2011).
21. Lovins (2011).
22. Kiron, Kruschwitz, Haanaes, Reeves, and Goh (2013).

Chapter 5

1. Zhexembayeva (2012).
2. Personal communication with Mark Vachon, vice president of ecoimagination at GE, July 19, 2011.
3. See https://us.walmart.mysustainabilityplan.com
4. May (2012).
5. Hagel (2010).
6. Kotter and Rathgeber (2005).
7. See http://www.naturalstep.org

Chapter 6

1. Cagnin, Loveridge, and Butler (2005).
2. Curtis (2012).
3. Upton (2011).

Glossary

1. See http://www.gartner.com/it-glossary/data-center-infrastructure-management-dcim
2. Lovins (2011), p. 178.
3. See http://www.webopedia.com/TERM/V/virtualization.html
4. For more details, see http://www.wbcsd.org/vision2050.aspx

References

American Society of Heating, Refrigerating and Air-Conditioning Engineers (ASH-RAE). (2011). *2011 Thermal guidelines for data processing environments—Expanded data center classes and usage guidance*. New York, NY:ASHRAE.

Aston, A. (2012, Janaury 24). *Why the Big Apple can be the world's first VERGE city*. Retrieved from Greenbiz.com Blog: http://www.greenbiz.com/blog/2012/01/24/why-big-apple-can-be-worlds-first-verge-city?page=full

ASU News. (2012, October 12). *Study maps greenhouse gas emissions to building, street level for U.S. cities*. Retrieved from ASU News Online: https://asunews.asu.edu/20121009_Hestia

Bartlett, D. (2011, November 15). *Listening to buildings*. Retrieved from Greenbiz.com: http://www.greenbiz.com/video/2011/11/15/listening-buildings-david-barlett

Cagnin, C. H., Loveridge, D., & Butler, J. (2005). *Business Sustainability Maturity Model*. Business Strategy and The Environment Conference 2005, September 4–6, 2005, Devonshire Hall, University of Leeds, Leeds, UK.

Cappuccio, D. J. (2010). *DCIM: Going beyond IT*. Boston, MA: Gartner.

Carter, D. (2011, October 1). *On the road to susainability: Listening to IBM's 'building whipserer'*. Retrieved from MT Online: http://www.mt-online.com/component/content/article/302-october2011/1915-on-the-road-to-sustainability-listening-to-ibms-building-whisperer.html

Curtis, S. (2012, November 22). *Data centre maturity model: Providing a holistic view of sustainability*. Retrieved from Techworld: http://features.techworld.com/data-centre/3412685/data-centre-maturity-model-providing-a-holistic-view-of-sustainability/

Ehrenfeld, J. (2008). *Sustainability by design*. New Haven, CT: Yale University Press.

Emerson Network Power. (2012). *The Cascade Effect*. Retrieved October 14, 2012, from Emerson Network Power: http://www.emersonnetworkpower.com/en-US/Latest-Thinking/EDC/EnergyLogic/Pages/CascadeEffect.aspx

Environmental Leader. (2012a, January 12). *IBM, 1E, Verdiem 'best in breed' for PC power management*. Retrieved from Environmental Leader: http://www.environmentalleader.com/2012/01/12/ibm-1e-verdiem-best-in-breed-for-pc-power-management/

Environmental Leader. (2012b, June 9). *Nike, Random Hacks of Kindess partner on online sustainable materials tool*. Retrieved from Environmental Leader:

http://www.environmentalleader.com/2012/06/08/nike-random-hacks-of-kindess-partner-on-online-sustainable-materials-tool/

Environmental Leader. (2012c, August 7). *Lucid software in Starbucks energy trial.* Retrieved from Environmental Leader: http://www.environmentalleader.com/2012/08/07/lucid-software-in-starbucks-energy-trial/

Forhez, M. (2008, November 11). *Tips for sustainable and optimized logisitcs.* Retrieved from CGT Conumer Goods Technology: http://consumergoods.edgl.com/trends/Tips-for-Sustainable-and-Optimized-Logistics51009

Gallagher, S. (2013, April 9). *Mobile cloud sucks power grid harder than datacenters.* Retrieved from Ars Technica: http://arstechnica.com/information-technology/2013/04/mobile-cloud-sucks-power-grid-harder-than-data-centers/

Ghandi, A. (2012). Are sleep states effective in data centers? In *IGCC '12 Proceedings of the 2012 International Green Computing Conference* (pp. 1–10). Washington, DC: IEEE Computer Society.

Granatstein, S. (Producer). (2008, November 9). *Following the trail of toxic e-waste.* Available from: http://www.cbsnews.com/2102-18560_162-4579229.html

Hagel, J. (2010). The power of pull: How small moves, smartly made, can set big things in motion. New York, NY: Basic Books.

Harris, D. (2012a, July 20). Hey, Los Angeles, Xerox thinks it can clear traffic on I-10. Retrieved from Gigaom.com: http://gigaom.com/2012/07/20/hey-los-angeles-xerox-thinks-it-can-clear-traffic-on-i-10/

Harris, D. (2012b, August 30). Managing sewage like traffic thanks to data. Retrieved from Gigaom.com: http://gigaom.com/2012/08/30/managing-sewage-like-traffic-thanks-to-data/

Hewlett-Packard. (2013). The disruption. Retrieved April 10, 2013, from http://thedisruption.com

Kiron, D., Kruschwitz, N., Haanaes, K., Reeves, M., & Goh, E. (2013, February). *The innovation bottom line.* Cambridge, MA: MIT Sloan Management Review.

Kotter, J., & Rathgeber, H. (2005). *Our iceberg is melting: Changing and succeeding under any conditions.* New York, NY: St. Martin's Press.

Lovins, A. B. (2011). *Reiventing fire: Bold business solutions for the new energy era.* Wind River Junction, VT: Chelsea Green Publishing Company.

May, M. (2012, November 28). *Healthcare kaizen: 5 questions with Mark Graban.* Retrieved from Matthew May's blog: http://matthewemay.com/2012/11/28/healthcare-kaizen-5-questions-with-mark-graban/

Pfeiffer, C. (2011, April 6). *Data center infrastructure management: A new tool for disaster recovery planning and response.* Retrieved from *Disaster Recovery Journal:* http://www.drj.com/articles/online-exclusive/data-center-infrastructure-management-a-new-tool-for-disaster-recovery-planning-and-response.html

Siegel, R. (2011, October 19). *Reducing carbon footprints in the transportation portion of the supply chain*. Retrieved from Triplepundit.com: http://www.triplepundit.com/reducing-carbon-footprints-transportation-portion-supply-chain/

Senge, P. (2010). *The necessary revolution: How individuals and organizations are working together to create a sustainable world*. New York, NY: Crown Business.

Tweed, K. (2012, September 11). *Doing the dirty work: Urjanet gathers energy data*. Retrieved from Greentech Media: http://www.greentechmedia.com/articles/read/doing-the-dirty-work-urjanet-gathers-energy-data

Upton, S. (2011, April). *Sustainable ICT—Action planning for the new economy*. Retrieved from Innovation Value Institute: http://ivi.nuim.ie/sites/ivi.nuim.ie/files/publications/SICTBookletfinal%20S%20Upton.pdf

U.S. Department of Energy. (2010). *2010 Building technologies program, Commerical Building Initiative*. Washington, DC: U.S. Department of Energy.

Werbach, A. (2009). *Strategy for sustainability: A business manifesto*. Boston, MA: Harvard Business Press.

Wikipedia. (n.d.). *Orchestration (computing)*. Retrieved July 18, 2012, from Wikipedia: http://en.wikipedia.org/wiki/Orchestration_(computing)

Willard, B. (2012). *The new sustainability advantage: Seven business case benefits of a triple bottom line* (10th ed.). New York, NY: New Society Publlishers.

World Business Council for Sustainable Development. (2010). *Vision 2050: The new agenda for business*. Conches-Geneva: WBCSD.

Yarger, H. R. (2010). *Towards a theory of strategy: Art lykke and the army war college strategy model*. Carlisle, PA: Strategic Studies Institute of the US Army War College.

Zhexembayeva, N. (2012, April 1). In *search of a new Cinderella story*. Retrieved from Managing Sustainability blog: http://www.2degreesnetwork.com/groups/managing-sustainability/resources/2degrees-bookclub-part-1-search-new-cinderella-story/#.T3m5fVB33-g.facebook

Index

OTHER TITLES IN ENVIRONMENTAL AND SOCIAL SUSTAINABILITY FOR BUSINESS ADVANTAGE COLLECTION

Chris Laszlo, Case Weatherhead School of Management
and Robert Sroufe, Duquesne University

- *Strategy Making in Nonprofit Organizations: A Model and Case Studies* by Jyoti Bachani and Mary Vradelis
- *Developing Sustainable Supply Chains to Drive Value: Management Issues, Insights, Concepts, and Tools* by Robert Sroufe and Steven Melnyk
- *A Primer on Sustainability: In the Business Environment 11/30/2013* by Ronald M. Whitfield and Jeanne McNett
- *The Thinking Executive's Guide to Sustainability 12/1/2013* by Kerul Kassel
- *Change Management for Sustainability 12/31/2013* by Houng Ha

FORTHCOMING TITLES ALSO IN OUR GIVING VOICE TO VALUES ON BUSINESS ETHICS AND CORPORATE SOCIAL RESPONSIBILITY COLLECTION

Mary Gentile, Babson College

- *Corporate Social Responsibility in the Chemical Industry: A Guide to Planning and Implementing Successful CSR Strategies 3/15/2014* by Barabara Burchi
- *Leadership Ethics: Moral Power for Business Leaders 4/15/2014* by Lindsay Thompson
- *Business Ethics: A Moral Reasoning Framework 6/15/2014* by Annabel Beerel
- *How to Foster a Culture of Ethics in Your Sports Organization: Ethical Traps and Making Better Choices in Sport 6/15/2014*
- *Responsible Corporate Communication: A Values-based Approach 7/1/2014* by David L. Remund

Announcing the Business Expert Press Digital Library

Concise E-books Business Students Need
for Classroom and Research

This book can also be purchased in an e-book collection by your library as
- a one-time purchase,
- that is owned forever,
- allows for simultaneous readers,
- has no restrictions on printing, and
- can be downloaded as PDFs from within the library community.

Our digital library collections are a great solution to beat the rising cost of textbooks. e-books can be loaded into their course management systems or onto student's e-book readers.

The **Business Expert Press** digital libraries are very affordable, with no obligation to buy in future years. For more information, please visit **www.businessexpertpress.com/librarians**. To set up a trial in the United States, please contact **Adam Chesler** at *adam.chesler@businessexpertpress.com* for all other regions, contact **Nicole Lee** at *nicole.lee@igroupnet.com*.

www.ingramcontent.com/pod-product-compliance
Lightning Source LLC
Chambersburg PA
CBHW071839200326
41519CB00016B/4175